Consciousness and Experience

Consciousness and Experience

William G. Lycan

A Bradford Book

The MIT Press

Cambridge, Massachusetts

London, England

This book was set in Sabon by Graphic Composition and was printed and bound in the United States of America.

First printing, 1996.

Library of Congress Cataloging-in-Publication Data

Lycan, William G.
  Consciousness and experience / William G. Lycan.
        p.   cm.
  Includes bibliographical references and index.
  ISBN 0-262-12197-2 (hc : alk. paper)
    1. Consciousness. 2. Experience. I. Title.
B808.9.L83   1996
126—dc20   95-48930
                                                          CIP

In memory of William Hiram Lycan, 1903–1994, but for whom I would never have become a philosopher, even though he hoped I would be a chemist

For her, consciousness itself was the deepest mystery. Here, on the first Sunday in October, a miracle was being enacted for her—the sky, the cedars, the lawn—merely because she had two round moist lumps the size of grapes connected by tenuous sinews to the nervous system.

A. N. Wilson, *Love Unknown*

Contents

Preface

In 1987, thanks also to the MIT Press, I published a work entitled *Consciousness*. In it I claimed to have saved the materialist view of human beings from all perils (real or apparent) looming from the general direction of conscious experience, subjectivity, qualia, and the phenomenal character of sensation. I still believe that I accomplished that feat, give or take a peril.

But not everyone has been convinced. In most cases this is due to plain pigheadedness. But in others it results from what I now see to have been badly compressed and cryptic exposition, and in still others it is articulately grounded in the peril or two that I inadvertently left unaddressed. My purposes in this book are to correct the latter two faults and to develop and ramify my theory of consciousness.

It seems that there is also a terminological problem: at least two reviewers of my previous book have emphatically complained that its title was false advertising and that it is not about *consciousness* at all, despite its offering accounts of conscious awareness (chapter 6), subjectivity and/or perspectivalness (chapter 7), "what it's like" (chapter 7), and qualia and phenomenal feels (chapter 8). Though I insist on keeping all these issues and further close relatives sharply separate from each other—as I shall strongly reemphasize here—I am baffled as to just what matter of "consciousness"

I am supposed to have ignored; neither reviewer troubled to say. But in this book I will try to be clearer about terms and taxonomy.

In his own review of *Consciousness,* Jeffrey Sicha likened me to Ahab, "fending off attacks on [my] philosophical Pequod, harpoon in hand" (1991, 554)—the idea being that I was too heavily engaged against antagonists to expound and develop my positive views in an orderly fashion. Well, yes and no, and no, and yes. I did take pains to formulate my "homuncular functionalist" version of materialism and to exhibit its distinctive strengths in handling problems of consciousness. But I also left too much detail unexplained. I did contend that homunctionalism is a secure and well-defended theory of the mind and that extant consciousness- and qualia-based objections to it are fairly easily repelled. But I overlooked two recent objections that do demand discussion; I will deal with these objections respectively in chapters 3 and 6 below.

Let me reiterate the dialectical position I set out at more length in the Epilogue to *Consciousness:* Many people think that materialism, and functionalist theories of mind in particular, are threatened or even refuted outright by one or another fact about conscious experience: subjectivity, qualia, phenomenal character, or the like. Sometimes this view remains only a muttered suspicion, while at better times actual arguments have been formulated. To date, none of the latter eight or nine arguments has succeeded; they have proved fallacious or been shown to rest on false or question-begging assumptions. Moreover, I and others have offered detailed diagnoses of the fallacies and of the intuitions on which the arguments are based. Some of these diagnoses even show that if my version of functionalism is true, then precisely those fallacies and intuitions are to be expected. (Thus functionalism is not only unrefuted but confirmed by them.) Further fractious mutterings cannot be respected, though I am bound to address any new antifunctionalist argument that might actually present itself.

Happily, the arguments that have appeared most recently are useful. Though we can rebut them, we can also learn from them, gaining a more detailed positive view of the structure of the mind. This is the main task that I hope to accomplish in this book.

Acknowledgments

Chapter 1 was written during my tenure as a Fellow of the Center for Advanced Study in the Behavioral Sciences, for whose more than generous support I am immensely grateful. For additional funding I thank the National Endowment for the Humanities (no. RA-20037-88) and the Andrew W. Mellon Foundation.

Half of chapter 2 appeared under the title "Consciousness as Internal Monitoring, I," in J. E. Tomberlin (ed.), *Philosophical Perspectives,* vol. 9, *AI, Connectionism, and Philosophical Psychology* (Ridgeview Publishing, 1995); the whole was published in N. Block, O. J. Flanagan, and G. Güzeldere (eds.), *The Nature of Consciousness* (MIT Press). Chapter 3 is reprinted from J. Tomberlin (ed.), *Philosophical Perspectives,* vol. 4, *Action Theory and Philosophy of Mind* (Ridgeview Publishing, 1990). A longer version of chapter 5 has appeared under the title "A Limited Defense of Phenomenal Information," in T. Metzinger (ed.), *Conscious Experience* (Imprint Academic). One section of chapter 6 and most of chapter 7 will appear as part of "Layered Perceptual Representation," in the published proceedings of the Eighth SOFIA Conference, edited by E. Villanueva (Ridgeview Publishing).

Figure 7.1, on page 151, is reprinted by gracious permission of Dr. William H. Ittelson.

For comments on parts of earlier drafts and for extensive discussion, I thank Kathleen Akins, Ned Block, Dan Dennett, Fred Dretske, Chris Hill, Gil Harman, Sydney Shoemaker, Bob Stalnaker, Kim Sterelny, Ken Taylor, Michael Tye, and the exuberant members of my 1995 NEH Summer Seminar "Problems of Consciousness." I am especially grateful to Joe Levine, Georges Rey, David Rosenthal, and Bob Van Gulick, each of whom gave me particularly lavish and helpful comments on an entire draft.

Consciousness and Experience

Introduction: What Is "The" Problem of Consciousness?

Both in philosophy and in psychology "the problem of consciousness" is supposed to be very special. It is not just the mind-body problem; few theorists question the eventual truth of materialism in some form, but many see a deep principled difficulty for the materialist in giving a plausible account of "consciousness." Nor is it just the problem of *intentionality,* or mental aboutness, in particular, since intentional states need not be conscious in any sense at all.[1] It has to do with the internal or subjective character of experience, paradigmatically sensory experience, and how such a thing can be accommodated in, or even tolerated by, a materialist theory of the mind.

And it is a conceptual problem, not merely an empirical one—it is a "How could . . . possibly . . . " question, not merely a "How does . . . " question. Scientifically, there is felt to be a systematic, if not insuperable, obstacle to psychological research, and philosophically there is felt to be a conceptual tension between materialism and the phenomenal or subjective character of experience.

Now, if we are to understand "the" problem, we must have a clear sense of what is meant by "consciousness," "subjective," "phenomenal," and the rest. And until recently, such a sense has been sadly lacking. But even in the past few years, I will argue, it has been in a way even more garishly lacking. Namely, although any number of useful clarifications and distinctions have emerged in the literature, *they have only continued to be trampled*. From time to time philosophers have acknowledged and even articulated a multiplicity of meanings, especially of the term "consciousness," but the fact of the multiplicity has never properly been taken to heart. Both psychologists and some philosophers still use the word univocally and without explication, as if it had one clear meaning and we all knew what it meant; many sharply distinct phenomena are still being lumped together under that heading and its commonly but falsely presumed synonyms, such as "subjectivity," "phenomenal character," and "qualia." The main purpose of this book is to argue that once we enforce the distinctions, we will be able to divide and conquer in a most promising manner.

1 CANDIDATES

Here are some importantly different uses of the word "conscious."

(1) *Organism consciousness*. A thing is a conscious *being* as opposed to a *non*conscious being if and only if (iff) it has the capacity for thought, sensation, feeling, etc. (whether or not that capacity is ever exercised).

(2) *Control consciousness*. A creature is conscious as opposed to *un*conscious iff it is awake, has occurrent mental states, and is in control of its actions in a way that is consonant with those mental states.

N.b., a person who is "unconscious" in this "control" sense can still be conscious *of* things, as in vivid dreams, and can also have *qualia* in any going sense of this term (which will be multiply disambiguated in chapter 4). Control consciousness is not too different from Ned Block's (1993, 1995) "access" consciousness, from David Rosenthal's (1991b) "creature" consciousness, or from Roger Shepard's (1991) "objective" consciousness.[2] This is a rough category, for there are lots of odd fringe cases here, e.g., that of somnambulism.

(3) *Consciousness of.* A creature is conscious (or aware) of this or that. The object of such consciousness may be external, abstract, physical, internal, somatic, mental, or whatever.

Note that this is a stronger notion than that of consciousness/awareness *that* something is the case, for one can be aware that x is F without being conscious/aware of x at the time (Dretske 1993).

(4) *State/event consciousness.* A state of a subject, or an event occurring within the subject, is a conscious state or event, as opposed to an unconscious or subconscious state or event, iff the subject is aware of being in the state or hosting the event.

There are at least three subcases of un- or subconsciousness in sense (4): simple distraction or other inattention; inaccessibility of processing, as in language understanding or pattern recognition; repression or some other Freudian mechanism.

(5) *Reportability.* In one useful sense, one is conscious of all and only those items on which one can readily issue a verbal report.

Putnam (1960), Rorty (1970), and Dennett (1978a) all mobilize versions of this notion. Though reportability can be accepted as a sometimes handy stipulation, I think it is not an *ordinary* sense of the term "consciousness," because it is both too easy and too hard to satisfy. For example, Putnam himself described a very dull automaton that, whenever it is in a particular state A, is simply caused then to print out the expression "I am in state A," but this is not an example of consciousness in any standard sense. Conversely, a creature might be conscious in almost any sense without having speech organs or even a module capable of driving such organs.[3]

(6) *Introspective consciousness.* This is "perception" by Lockean "inner sense," i.e., by focusing one's attention on the internal character of one's experience itself.

There are light and casual degrees of this, more deliberate degrees, and even very determined degrees amounting to serious phenomenological investigation. (Note how entirely independent sense (6) is of (1) and (2); beings could be conscious in both of those senses but lack introspection entirely.) I should mention—what will be explained at more length in the next chapter—that the metaphor of "inner perception" is only that, and is to be cashed in terms of empirically discoverable attention mechanisms that output representations of some of one's own psychological states.[4]

Very likely, introspective consciousness is a special case of (3), consciousness of, and arguably it explains (4), state/event consciousness (see chapter 2).

(7) *Subjective consciousness.* This is (metaphorically speaking) having a "point of view." A subject's consciousness in this sense is "what it is like" for the subject to be in whatever mental states it is in. A tighter characterization might be: what can be described, if at all, only in the first person.

I will argue in chapter 3 that this sort of consciousness is completely explained by (6), introspective consciousness.

(8) *Self-consciousness.* This is, at least, having a sense of oneself as an individual separate from other individuals and the rest of one's surroundings. In a stronger sense, it is consciousness *of* one's self.

(Whatever this might be, and if there is any. I would not touch this sense for a free week on Maui with champagne thrown in.[5])

There are more uses of "conscious." (And, of course, there are even more specialized and topic-tied uses: "altered states of consciousness," "false consciousness," social abstract-noun phrases such as "feminist consciousness" or "the religious consciousness of the age," and the like.)

Which uses are problematic in the seemingly special way? Uses (1) (organism consciousness) and (2) (control consciousness) involve no more than the mind-body problem itself. Uses (3) (consciousness of) and (4) (state/event consciousness) seem to be just special cases of intentionality. Use (5) (reportability) is not especially interesting, as its proponents have been concerned to point out. Use (6) (introspective consciousness) is no more troublesome than are ordinary modes of perception or attention mechanisms, however empirically difficult these might be (remember that "the" problem is not primarily an empirical one).

So we will be dealing primarily with consciousness in sense (7). (As I said, I refuse to touch sense (8).) But to have narrowed the topic down this far is, comparatively, to have narrowed it hardly at all, for further distinctions proliferate. Here are some possible candidates for "the" problem of consciousness (sense (7)).

(A)   *The subject/object distinction,* i.e., being in a mental state oneself versus observing someone else's brain while he or she is in that state. The felt mutual incongruity of these two conditions can psychologically lead to doubt about materialism.

I argued in *Consciousness* that one must guard against the "stereoptic [or stereoscopic]" fallacy of supposing that, because to have a vivid perceptual experience oneself is nothing like observing the brain of someone else who is having it, having such an experience must be entirely different in nature from any goings-on in the brain that underlie one's having it. (Even to call this inference a "fallacy" is to flatter it.)

(B) *Immediate or at least privileged access.* Almost no one would deny that I can both experience and know the contents of my own mind in a way that you can neither experience nor know the contents of my mind.

But this is not a *problem;* it is simply a fact, which must be explained, or at least accommodated, by any adequate theory of the mind.

(C) *Temporal and other empirical anomalies.* There are fascinating empirical but philosophically shocking puzzles about the relations between observationally detectable events and subjects' awareness of these events. (These are discussed at length by Dennett and Kinsbourne [1992a] and Dennett [1991]; see chapter 2 below.) Work on one version or another of the "binding problem" in brain science is also sometimes labeled as research on "consciousness" per se, as for example by Crick and Koch (1990).

(D) *How/why did consciousness evolve, and what is it for?* (Armstrong [1980], Van Gulick [1989, 1994], Dennett [1991], and especially Flanagan [1992] have all offered conjectures on this.)

(E) *Epistemology,* e.g., of "inverted spectrum." How could we possibly tell whether someone's internal color spectrum is inverted, or whether a food sample tastes the same to one person who likes it and to another who does not?

Candidates (C) through (E) are interesting and perhaps intractable problems for psychophysical research, but unless one is a verificationist, one will not see great philosophical significance in them.

(F)   *"Inverted qualia" and "absent qualia," or zombie, arguments.* To some philosophers it has seemed obvious that the conditions of this or that materialist theory of conscious experience could be fulfilled and yet the organism in question have either inverted phenomenal contents or no conscious or phenomenal experience at all.

Such arguments are most often aimed against functionalist versions of materialism. (The issues here are metaphysical as opposed to epistemological, as in (E).) In chapters 3 and 5 of *Consciousness* I accepted a few of these arguments, aimed against simpleminded materialist theories that I do not hold, but put the rest down to their proponents' hyperactive imagination. I will revisit some of these issues in chapter 6 below.

2   MORE SERIOUS BUT STILL DIVERSE CANDIDATES

Candidates (A) and (B) are nonproblems. Candidates (C), (D), and (E) are at least not "the" big conceptual problem. Candidate (F) comprehends a family of parallel arguments by counterexample against various materialist theories of the mind (as I said, I believe that some of the counterexamples work and some do not), but the arguments are purely negative, and even where they do work, they do little by themselves to bring out what "the" big problem is supposed to be.

Now focus introspectively on the phenomenal character of your inner experience, say on the rich cyan color presented to you by the background on your new state-of-the-art color monitor, and some bigger conceptual difficulties will bare their teeth.

(G)   *Homogeneity or grainlessness.* Some theorists, most notably Sellars (1962, 1965, 1971) have seen a severe incongruity between the smooth continuous character of a phenomenal quality such as color—phenomenal pink is simply "pink through and through," in Sellars's phrase—and the discrete, particulate nature of the material of which we are made.

This can be written off by materialists as a threshold effect, simply a matter of the subject's failure to perceive the gaps that make for grain. As Armstrong (1968a) would say, we mistake our failure to perceive gaps for a successful perceiving that there are no gaps. But the matter of homogeneity is extraordinarily complicated, and, somewhat arbitrarily, I choose not to engage it in this book.[6]

(H) *The monadic, first-order qualia of apparent phenomenal objects.* I contend that to a striking extent Russell was right: one's visual field, for example, does take the form of a mosaic, an array of irregularly shaped color patches fitting together, and we can talk extensively about each patch and its qualitative and relational properties.[7]

In particular, not only the cyan color presented by your monitor but also the yellow of Russell's famous second candle flame seem to be the colors of phenomenal *things*. If we are not simply to give up materialism in favor of a sense-datum metaphysics, this sort of qualia talk must be explicated in a naturalistically acceptable way, and that is no easy task. I argued in *Consciousness* that the objects are intentional objects, often unreal intentional inexistents; I will defend this theory further in chapter 4 below. And as we will see, a new and more rarefied use of the term "quale" has emerged in recent years, posing a new problem for the theory (see chapter 6).

To anticipate an important theme of this book, note that there is no obviously important relation between qualia in the strict sense of (H) and consciousness in any of our original senses of this term, save the uninteresting sense (1) (organism consciousness). In particular, one cannot simply assume that if a subject's state involves a quale, then the subject must be conscious or aware of being in that state or being acquainted with that quale.[8] One might go on to argue a connection between qualia in the present sense and some version of subjectivity or "what it's like," but here too one would *have* to argue it. I will say more of this in chapter 4.

(I)   *The intrinsic perspectival, point-of-view and/or first-person aspect of experience,* as discussed by Nagel (1974). This aspect is not just (A), the mere fact that, e.g., seeing cyan oneself is not like watching the gray cheesy brain of someone else who is seeing cyan, nor is it just the inevitable but entirely objective filtering of external information.

(J)   *Funny facts,* as revealed by the "knowledge arguments" given by Nagel (1974) and Jackson (1982). These facts cannot be scientific facts, for they can be known only from particular points of view, some of which may be inaccessible to human beings.

Candidates (I) and (J) are closely related, though not precisely the same problem. I addressed both in chapter 7 of *Consciousness;* I will do considerably better in chapter 3 below.

(K)   *Ineffability.* One often cannot express in words what it is like to have a particular sensation, except in comparative terms that can be understood only by someone who has had a closely related experience.

(L)   *The "explanatory gap,"* called to our attention by Levine (1983): even if God were to assure us that, say, the type-identity theory of mind is true and that such-and-such a conscious experience is strictly identical with a firing of certain neural fibers, we would still lack an explanation of why those fiber firings feel to their subjects in the distinctive way in which they do.

For example, granted that M-fiber firings do simply constitute their subject's being appeared to mauvely, *why* does this experience have the qualitative character of phenomenal mauve rather than some other such as phenomenal yellow?

Candidates (I) through (L) do call for some positive account, and I gave none in *Consciousness*. I will argue here that a good one is furnished by Locke's "inner sense" picture of introspection, coupled with the analogy with indexical utterances in natural languages that I will develop in chapter 3.

As I said in my preface, my strategy will be to divide and conquer. Once we keep (G) through (L) ruthlessly separate and tackle each set of issues on its own terms, we will see that each is tractable. I do not say that in each case my solution will be immune to objection; I do claim that my solutions are plausible and that they cannot easily be refuted.

I should emphasize that my goals are modestly limited to those sketched in the preceding paragraph: in sum, to show how it is possible and even plausible that a purely physical organism might exemplify unusual features of the sort that figure in (G) through (L), not just individually but all at once. I will not claim, here or ever, to "explain consciousness" (in the title phrase of Dennett's well-known work). For on my own view, that would be to explain each of any number of different things, a set of Herculean empirical and philosophical tasks. Also, as Joseph Levine has observed to me, it would also court a fallacy of composition, since the set of explanations of all the various phenomena might not yield a master explanation of their organic sum.

Some defenders of materialism like to start from a heavily fortified position, by conceding almost nothing to their consciousness- or subjectivity- or qualia-driven critics; they simply deny the early premises of their critics' arguments. I incline, temperamentally, in just the opposite direction. I would rather give the critics lots of rope, grant their early premises, and then, after making many concessions, show that the arguments fail anyway and that the hostile premises can triumphantly be welcomed within a master theory of consciousness, subjectivity, qualia, and the rest. In particular, I will concede, indeed insist, that the phenomenal characters of (some) mental states are

- real,
- internal,
- specially accessible to/by me,
- ineffable,
- intrinsically perspectival,
- in one sense, inaccessible to science,
- in one sense, inexplicable.

As we will see, each of these features is nicely predicted by the Lockean picture I have mentioned, with no implication that consciousness is a surd in nature or in any other way an obstacle to functionalist theories of mind.

I will also have another go at the subproject of establishing what I call the *hegemony of representation*. As in *Consciousness* (though I was insufficiently explicit about it at the time),[9] I am concerned to maintain a weak version of Brentano's doctrine that the mental and the intentional are one and the same. Weak, because I am not sure that intentionality suffices for representation, but my claim is strong enough: the mind has no special properties that are not exhausted by its representational properties, along with or in combination with the functional organization of its components. It would follow that once representation itself is (eventually) understood, then not only consciousness in our present sense but subjectivity, qualia, "what it's like," and every other aspect of the mental will be explicable in terms of representation together with the underlying functionally organized neurophysiology, without our positing any other ingredient not already well understood from the naturalistic point of view.

I do not think there will be any "problem of consciousness" left.

Conscious Awareness as Internal Monitoring

Locke put forward the theory of consciousness as "internal Sense" or "reflection"; Kant made it "inner sense, by means of which the mind intuits itself or its inner state."[1] On this theory, consciousness is a perceptionlike second-order representing of our own psychological states and events.

As we saw in chapter 1, the term "consciousness" has many distinct uses. My concern in this chapter is with sense (4) state/event consciousness, the use according to which much of one's mental or psychological activity is *un*conscious or subconscious, even when one is wide awake and well aware of other goings-on, both external and internal. I will argue that what distinguishes conscious mental activity from un- and subconscious mental activity is indeed second-order representing. Thus consciousness in sense (4) is to be subsumed under sense (6), introspective consciousness; though the senses are themselves distinct, I will argue that state/event consciousness is in fact a special case of, and is explained by, introspection.

Locke's idea has been urged in our own time by philosophers such as D. M. Armstrong (1968b, 1980) and psychologists such as Bernard Baars (1983, 1988); I also defended it in chapter 6 of *Consciousness*. But some interesting criticisms have been raised against the view by a number of theorists. In this chapter I will rebut a few; I am particularly concerned to overcome an objection due to Georges Rey (1983, 1988).

1 THE LOCKEAN THEORY AND ITS ACCOMPLISHMENTS

Armstrong states the inner-sense doctrine as follows. "Introspective consciousness . . . is a perception-like awareness of current states and activities in our own mind. The current activities will include sense-perception: which latter is the awareness of current states and activities of our environment and our body" (1980, 61). As I would put it, consciousness is the functioning of internal *attention mechanisms* directed at lower-order psychological states and events. I would also add (or make more explicit) a soupçon of teleology: attention mechanisms are devices that have the *job* of relaying and/or coordinating information about ongoing psychological events and processes.[2]

Armstrong offers a plausible Just-So Story to explain the prevalence of introspective consciousness:

The biological function of introspective consciousness . . . is to sophisticate our mental processes in the interests of more sophisticated action.

Inner perception makes the sophistication of our mental processes possible in the following way. If we have a faculty that can make us aware of current mental states and activities, then it will be much easier to achieve *integration* of the states and activities, to get them working together in the complex and sophisticated ways necessary to achieve complex and sophisticated ends.

. . . Co-ordination [of many parallel processes] can only be achieved if the portion of the computing space made available for administering the overall plan is continuously made "aware" of the current mental state of play with respect to the lower-level operations that are running in parallel. Only with this feedback is control possible. . . . It is no accident that fully alert introspective consciousness characteristically arises in *problem* situations, situations that standard routines cannot carry one through. (1980, 65–66)[3]

A slightly deflated version of this idea will figure in my own defense of the inner-sense theory.

I should repeat and emphasize that my concern in this chapter is solely with the notion of conscious awareness, with the distinction between conscious mental states and un-, sub-, pre-, or otherwise nonconscious mental states. In particular, here I am not addressing issues of qualia or phenomenal character, which I will resolve (almost) entirely satisfactorily later on. There may be inner-sense theorists who believe that their views solve problems of qualia; I make no such claim, for I think that qualia problems and the nature of conscious awareness are mutually independent and indeed have little to do with each other.[4] (I will argue for this stark independence in chapter 4, where we turn to qualia proper.)

The inner-sense view of consciousness has a number of advantages, the first of which is that it does distinguish awareness from mere psychology, and conscious states/ events (in the sense indicated above) from mere mentation. We may plausibly suppose that many lower animals have psychologies and mentation, or at least internal representation, without awareness. Second, the view affords some *grades* of un- or subconsciousness, e.g., a state/event may be unconscious just because it is unattended, but a Freudian wish to kill one's father may have been rendered unattend*able* by some masterful Censor.[5] And further distinctions are available, both for animals and for human beings.

Third, the inner-sense account affords the best solution I know to the problem of subjectivity and "knowing what it's like," raised by B. A. Farrell (1950), Thomas Nagel (1974), and Frank Jackson (1982). Georges Rey (1991, 1992) and I (Lycan 1990) hit upon that solution independently a few years ago (though Rey does not think of his own second-order representations as deliverances of "inner sense"). It involves the behavior of indexical terms in the proprietary vocabulary mobilized by the relevant attention mechanisms. I will expound it again in chapter 3.

Fourth, the inner-sense view sorts out a longstanding issue about sensations and feeling. Consider pain. A minor pain may go unfelt, or so we sometimes say.[6] Even quite a bad pain may not be felt if attention is distracted by sufficiently pressing concerns. Yet such assertions as my last two can sound anomalous; as David Lewis once said, meaning to tautologize, "pain is a feeling." When one person's commonplace sounds to another contradictory on its face, we should suspect equivocation, and the inner-sense model delivers: Sometimes the word "pain" is used to mean just the first-order representation of damage or disorder, a representation that can go unnoticed. But sometimes "pain" means a conscious feeling or mode of awareness, and on this usage the phrase "unfelt pain" is simply self-contradictory; it comprehends both the first-order representation and the second-order scanning together. Thus the equivocation that gave rise to the issue. The issue is dissolved.

The inner-sense theory as I have formulated it makes at least one brutally empirical commitment: to the actual existence of internal attention mechanisms in our brains. And so it may and should be wondered[7] whether the theory has received any scientific confirmation, be it cognitive-psychological or neurophysiological. I did give some cognitive references in *Consciousness* (Broadbent 1958, 1982; Neisser 1967; Lackner and Garrett 1973; Parasuraman and Davies 1984; Johnston and Dark 1986), though certainly more evidence would be better. But in advance, I think we have at least one good a priori reason for confidence that the internal attention mechanisms are there to be found. It is that our introspective attention is under voluntary control. I can ask you to concentrate on your visual field as such, then focus on a particular patch of red, then shift your attention to the upper left quadrant of the field, etc., and you can do those things at will, with a remarkable degree of facility and precision. Something cognitive, and presumably something neurophysiological, subserve this ability.

2 FALLIBILITY

The preceding point reveals a consequence of the Inner Sense theory that may disturb, namely, that since an internal monitor is a physical device, and so subject to malfunction, it might report falsely; the very fallibility of monitoring guarantees that a subject might register a first-order event incorrectly. Thus the inner-sense theory implies an appearance/reality distinction for subjectivity.

A Cartesian incorrigibilist would be appalled, of course. So would the Cartesian's unlikely bedfellow, the Wittgensteinian incorrigibilist. Neither such animal abounds nowadays, thanks to the decline of Cartesian doctrine generally, the weakening of Wittgensteinian "conceptual truths," and Armstrong's specific arguments against incorrigibility of both sorts (1968b, 100–115);[8] it is generally conceded that one can or in theory might mistake and misdescribe the contents of one's own experience. Yet the inner-sense view has three further implications that may be more troubling to the contemporary reader.

First, it seems to follow from the inner-sense theory that there could be creatures who have pains but are never aware of them. Shoemaker (1994b) deplores this. Though he grants that pain can "occasionally" escape awareness, he insists that such could not happen "as a matter of course; it may be true in Lake Wobegon that all of the children are above average, but it can't be true everywhere" (1994b, 273–274).

Although unfelt pains cannot occur as a matter of course, he does not say why they can still occur occasionally; pain and awareness afford no obvious analogue of the concept of average.)

Massive unawareness of pain is probably nomologically impossible for organisms like us, in whom pain hooks up with cognition and conation is complex ways. It may well be nomologically impossible for organisms of any very complicated kind, since a system of internal monitoring may be required for any such beast to succeed in the real world. At worst, the inner-sense theory implies that Shoemaker's pain-blind creatures are metaphysically possible. So he must take on the daunting task of showing that they are not even metaphysically possible.

His strategy is to show that if the creatures are unaware of their pains, then they must be unaware of a good deal else besides: since "pain is a feeling," they feel the pains, and the pains are unpleasant, and they dislike the pains and want them to cease. If the latter desire has anything like its normal causal role, the creatures should take action, such as downing aspirin and calling the doctor. But such behavior is "intelligible *as* pain behavior only on the assumption that the subject is aware of pain; for to see [it] *as* pain behavior is to see [it] as motivated by such states of the creature as the belief that it is in pain, the desire to be rid of the pain, and the belief that such and such a course of behavior will achieve that result." So the pains of which our creatures are unaware cannot have the standard features that make a state a pain, QED.

Unlike Shoemaker, I think it is an entirely empirical question which parts of the pain-behavior syndrome are caused by the first-order pain condition and which by second-order awareness of the condition. Certainly a human being can engage in some pain behavior, such as limping or favoring, while remaining unaware of the pain. And anecdotally, it seems that if sufficiently distracted, a subject can pain-behave fairly violently, and even cry out, while still un-aware of the pain. Other, more sophisticated forms of pain behavior, such as calling the doctor and minutely describing the pain, presumably require awareness.

So probably the creatures' pain-behavior syndrome would differ to some degree from that of normal human be-ings. (And, of course, they would not have "pains" at all in the composite sense credited above to David Lewis.) Are these still pains in the first-order sense? Shoemaker goes on to concede that a state could play part of the standard role of pain—"its being caused by . . . bodily damage of various sorts . . . and its causing behaviors, such as winces, grimaces and moans, that can be involuntary and do not have to be ra-tionalized," but he stolidly declares that such a state "would not be pain. Indeed, it would not be a mental state at all" (1994b, 275).

Obviously, I disagree. Shoemaker seems to be running together the two senses of "pain" distinguished in the previ-ous section (witness his echo of Lewis's "pain is a feeling"). Of course, it is impossible for any creature (ever) to have a pain in the strong, composite sense and yet remain unaware of it. But Shoemaker seems to admit that our pain-blind crea-tures can have pains in the weaker, first-order sense; he just chooses to withhold the word. Ordinary usage rebukes him.

The second potentially disturbing implication of the inner-sense theory is that in addition to misreporting the character of a first-order state, an internal monitor could in principle fire without anything like a proper cause, giving a false positive. Thus the inner-sense view predicts that it is possible for a person to be unveridically conscious or aware of a sensation that simply does not exist. You might intro-spect a sharp, severe pain when there is in fact no pain at all.

I am happy to live with this theoretical possibility. No-tice, first, that it is not as *conceptually* anomalous as it sounds. My description misleadingly suggests that you might feel as if in severe pain, with everything that is involved in feeling a severe pain, which would include all the first-order functional effects of the pain—withdrawal, wincing, involuntary crying out, favoring, and the like—while having no actual pain whatever. That suggestion is, I agree, truly weird. But it is not in fact a consequence of the inner-sense theory. If (as the present hypothesis has it) there is no first-order pain sensation at all but merely a mendacious representation of one, there is no reason to think that all or any of these usual functional effects would indeed ensue. You would be introspecting something that had some of the qualitative aspects of a pain, but important elements would be missing; you might be in the position of the morphine patients, who manifest "reactive dissociation," saying that they still feel the pain as intensely as ever but no longer mind it. (Remember that on my view, introspective awareness itself is just one of several normal effects of a first-order pain sensation, and is largely independent of the sensation's other normal effects.)

Besides, the mere theoretical possibility of the false positive does not mean that such things can happen easily. *Perhaps* they do happen, as when an apprehensive child or medical patient mistakes a light touch or a sensation of cold for a pain, but those examples are usually mistaken perceptions of actual sensations. It is at best rare for a person to be aware of a pain but give no behavioral or other functional sign of pain. I suspect that our introspectors are well wired and virtually never fire for no reason at all. It is not as though they were external sense organs, prey to predictable perceptual illusions and at the mercy of unusual environmental setups. The first-order sectors they scan are immured right there in the brain with them, and there is little to threaten the informational connection (though one must never underestimate the power of drugs or lesions to sever what are normally very tight psychological connections: Wittgensteinian "conceptual truths" about mental states are often counterexampled by unusual clinical conditions).

In making these two replies to the objection from false positives, I have used the vernacular of "felt" and "unfelt pains," i.e., the terminology that applies "pain" to the first-order representation of damage or disorder without requiring introspective awareness of that representation. If instead one prefers the more comprehensive use of "pain," then one will be frustrated in trying to use the term, for a false positive will not count as pain in this inclusive sense but will merely feel like pain, or have the introspective component of pain without the first-order sensory component. Perhaps we should now recognize a third sense of "pain," meaning just the introspective awareness (as) of pain, whether or not that awareness is veridical. In this third sense, trivially, your feeling pain guarantees that there is pain, even if there is no first-order representation of disorder. (On the other hand, as against acknowledging the third sense, remember that an unveridical awareness of pain would not be accompanied by the other usual effects of the first-order sensation and would probably not be phenomenally very like veridical awareness of pain. Knowing oneself to be the victim of a false positive, one might or might not be moved to call one's state of awareness "pain"; this is something we cannot tell until we have documented and investigated an actual false-positive case, for we would need some introspective help from the victim even if we could not take everything he or she said at face value.)

The third potentially disturbing implication of the inner-sense theory was recently noted (in a different connection, as will be discussed in section 7 below) by Dennett (1991, 132–133). He raises the question of second-order seeming: "the bizarre category of the objectively subjective—the way things actually, objectively seem to you even if they don't seem to seem that way to you!" He thereupon "brusquely denies the possibility in principle of consciousness of a stimulus in the absence of the subject's belief in that consciousness." But the inner-sense view affords a perfect model of just such a state of affairs: a first-order state is conscious in virtue of being scanned, and it seems a certain way to its subject, but the scanning is not itself scanned. This would be precisely a case of being conscious of a stimulus without the subject's believing in that consciousness. Moreover, a second-order monitor could break down and make a first-order state seem to seem to me in a way that the state does not, in fact, seem to me.

Dennett calls this idea "metaphysically dubious" as well as impossible in principle. But his only argument, based on "first-person operationalism," is as follows:

Opposition to this operationalism appeals, as usual, to possible facts beyond the ken of the operationalist's test, but now the operationalist is the subject himself, so the objection backfires: "Just because you can't tell, by your preferred ways, whether or not you were conscious of x, that doesn't mean you weren't. Maybe you were conscious of x but just can't find any evidence for it!" Does anyone, on reflection, really want to say that? Putative facts about consciousness that swim out of reach of both "outside" and "inside" observers are strange facts indeed. (Dennett 1991, 132–133)

Well. Just to gratify Dennett's rhetorical curiosity: yes, I, on reflection, really want to say that, or rather, to insist on its perfect coherence as a factual possibility. Since the inner-sense theory provides an excellent model for the second-order situation that appalls Dennett and since the theory may well be true, the second-order situation is without question a genuine possibility. (Remember, if the inner-sense theory is false, this is a brutely empirical fact; certainly Mother Nature could have equipped us with banks of first- and second-order internal monitors, whether or not she did in fact choose to do so.) As for the strange aquatic facts, I see no reason to grant that they do "swim out of reach of" the outside observers, at least since in principle a neuroscientist could observe a first-order state being scanned by an unscanned monitor and know just what was going on.

As before, I agree that the notion of an appearance/reality distinction for conscious awareness is odd on its face, and I am inclined to think that dramatic cases of an appearance/reality gap are rare and pathological, but I see here no powerful objection to the inner-sense view.[9]

3 TERMINOLOGY

In correspondence, Fred Dretske has asked a good pair of questions about the inner-sense theory:[10] Why is consciousness (or just representation) *of* certain physical states enough to make these states *themselves* "conscious"? And more specifically, what is so special about physical states of this sort that consciousness of them makes them—but not just any old physical state—conscious? After all, we are conscious *of* (what are in fact) physical states of our stomachs; for that matter, through ordinary perception we are conscious of physical states of our skins, such as their being freckled, but no one would distinguish between "conscious" and "unconscious" stomachs, or between "conscious" and "unconscious" frecklednesses.

Indeed, why does the concept work in this way (assuming that it does work in this way)? It may have something historically to do with the fact that until the twentieth century the mental/psychological was simply identified with the conscious, and so only recently have we had to adopt a taxonomic distinction between states we are aware of holding and states we are not. (I am assuming that there is such a distinction in reality, and I believe—what is not uncontroversial—that the distinction in theory applies to any ordinary mental state, not counting states already described as "being consciously aware of [so-and-so]."

What is it that is so special about physical states of this sort that consciousness *of* them makes them conscious? That they are themselves mental. Stomachs and freckled patches of skin are not mental. It seems that psychological states are called "conscious states" when we are conscious of them, but nonpsychological things are not.

Given the reality of the distinction between states we are aware of being in and states we are not aware of being in, the only remaining question is, why the *word* "conscious" is thus dragged in as an adjective to mark it. My bet is that there is a grammatical answer. Maybe it is a transferred epithet: we began with the adverbial form, as in "consciously thought" or "consciously felt," and when we made the verb into a noun, the adverb automatically became an adjective—as in the move from "meditatively sipped" to "took a meditative sip." This is fairly plausible; at any rate, it is the best I can do for now.

In any case, it is important to see that the question pertains to the notion of conscious awareness itself; it is not a problem for, or objection to, the inner-sense theory of awareness in particular.

Dretske makes a related, ostensibly more substantive criticism of the theory as I have stated it. He argues at some length that there is a sense of "conscious" in which, as he oxymoronically puts it, "an experience can be conscious without anyone—including the person having it—being conscious of having it" (Dretske 1993, 263). As he says, this usage sounds "odd, perhaps even contradictory, to those philosophers who . . . embrace an inner spotlight view of consciousness" (as targets he cites Armstrong, Rosenthal, and me in particular). In brief, his argument is that to perceive anything, whether or not one is conscious of doing that perceiving, is to be conscious of the thing perceived, and thus is to be "in a conscious state of some sort." (He notes that Armstrong for one actually agrees in principle, for Armstrong (1980, 59) grants a sense in which any perceiver *eo ipso* enjoys "perceptual consciousness," whether or not he or she is conscious or aware of the perceiving itself. Thus, the inner-sense or "inner spotlight" view has gone wrong, at least in its implication that for a state to be a conscious state, its subject must be aware of being in it.

Here I believe the issue is purely verbal. Although I cannot myself hear a natural sense of the phrase "conscious state" other than as meaning "state one is conscious of being in," the philosophical use of "conscious" is by now well and truly up for grabs, and the best one can do is to be as clear as possible in one's technical specification.[11] Let us grant, then, a sense, whether natural or merely technical, in which a state of perceiving is a conscious state, whether or not its subject is conscious of being in it. However, I will not resist remarking that Dretske's and Armstrong's usage has the vice of making Armstrong's own term "perceptual consciousness" redundant; the occurrence of "consciousness" within it is gratuitous. Also, we need no special *theory* of consciousness in the perceptual sense, since a theory of "perceptual consciousness" would just be a theory of perception itself and its intentionality.[12] But the inner-sense theory of consciousness is not, and has never pretended to be, a theory of "perceptual consciousness" in Dretske's and Armstrong's sense. It is (please forgive the repetition) a theory of conscious awareness, of "conscious states" in my original sense of states that one is conscious of being in.

Dretske adds a more specific objection to the inner-sense theory. Distinguishing between awareness of things, which is referentially transparent, and awareness of facts, which presupposes mobilization of particular concepts, he argues as follows (Dretske 1993, 279–280). Suppose that a person has two experiences, E(Alpha) and E(Beta), that differ subtly in their contents, and the person does introspect the two but fails to register the difference (compare Rock 1983, 53–57). If the person is merely "thing-aware" of a first-order psychological state without being "fact-aware" of the state, and if his thing-awareness is supposed to constitute the state's being a conscious state, then his

> failure to realize, [her/his] total unawareness of the fact *that* there is a difference between E(Alpha) and E(Beta), is irrelevant to whether there is a conscious difference between these two experiences. This being so, the "inner sense" theory of what makes a mental state conscious does nothing to *improve* one's epistemic access to one's own conscious states. . . . What good is an inner spotlight, an introspective awareness of mental events, if it doesn't give one epistemic access to the events on which it shines? (Dretske 1993, 279–280)

(Further, the inner-sense theory "multiplies the problems by multiplying the facts of which we are not aware.")

This is puzzling on its face, since the topic of epistemic access arises rather suddenly; the inner-sense account was offered as a theory of the conscious/nonconscious distinction in our original sense, not as a contribution to epistemology. Besides, introspection conceived as inner perception normally does improve one's epistemic position, for although it is indeed possible for one to be thing-aware of a first-order state without being fact-aware of being in that state, thing-awareness will often directly *give rise to* fact-awareness, just as in the case of ordinary external perception.

I suspect that what motivated these remarks of Dretske's was the following: In the section of his paper that surrounds the present objection, Dretske is contrasting the inner-sense view with a close relative, David Rosenthal's (1986, 1990b, 1991b, 1992) "Higher-Order Thought" theory, which is also a major target of his essay, and it seems that Dretske means the objection comparatively. That is, I believe he means to say that if his original criticism is damaging to the higher-order-thought account, it refutes the inner-sense view even more decisively, thus: He has argued (correctly) that being the object of a higher-order thought is not what makes a state conscious in the sense of "perceptual consciousness." But at least a higher-order thought would make the state's subject aware *that* he or she was in that state, which is something. By contrast, a mere higher-order thing-awareness of the state would not, *eo ipso*, even yield such fact-awareness, and so is *completely* irrelevant to perceptual consciousness.[13]

If this interpretation of Dretske's objection is correct, the objection again simply goes wide of my own position. For again, I am using inner-sense to explicate conscious awareness, not "perceptual consciousness."

Dretske's point is of independent interest, however: Whatever the exact function(s) of introspection may be, we may be fairly sure that Mother Nature intended introspection to confer some cognitive benefit, and a theory of introspective awareness that masked this or made it unintelligible would be to this extent a bad theory. Dretske is right to insist that *mere* thing-awareness of a first-order state would be a cognitive idler. So I must reemphasize my presumption that internal monitoring normally or often does give rise to introspective belief, and I should also note that, again on the model of external perception, introspection presents its object under an aspect, *as* being a certain way. I will argue in chapters 3 and 5 below that such introspective aspects and "ways" are important, though ineffable.

4   ROSENTHAL AGAINST INNER SENSE

Rosenthal makes a direct argument against the inner-sense account (1990b; 1991b, 7–8).[14] It begins with the claim that "perceiving always involves some sensory quality." This claim might be taken by a naive inner-sense theorist to help explain the qualitative dimension of a conscious first-order sensory state: perhaps the first-order state is felt to have a qualitative or phenomenal aspect because it gives rise to an internal perception that itself "involves some sensory quality." But as Rosenthal briskly points out, in that way lies regress, for the sensory quality of the second-order state would remain to be explained.

The failure of the naive idea just mentioned is no embarrassment to my own inner-sense view, since that view bears no responsibility for explaining qualia or phenomenal character. But Rosenthal rides his initial claim further: if perceiving always involves some sensory quality and if internal monitoring is perceiving, then internal monitoring itself must indeed involve some sensory quality. A dilemma ensues. Either the quality is just the same quality as is exhibited by the first-order state being scanned, or it is some second, higher-order sensory quality. But the former is at best unmotivated and presumably false: "When we see a tomato, the redness of our sensation is not literally the same property as the redness of the tomato." And if the latter, "it's a mystery just what mental quality a higher-order perception could have. What mental qualities are available other than those we're conscious of when we're conscious of our first-order sensory states?"

My main reply to this is to reject the extending and the extension of Rosenthal's initial claim to internal monitoring itself. The inner-sense theorist does not contend (at least neither Armstrong nor I contend) that internal monitoring is like external perception in every single respect. And in particular, we should not expect internal monitoring to share the property of involving some presented sensory quality at its own level of operation. For the sensory properties presented in first-order states are, according to me (*Consciousness*, chap. 8), the represented features of physical objects;

e.g., the color presented in a (first-order) visual perception is the represented color of a physical object. First-order states themselves do not have ecologically significant features of the sort physical objects do, and so we would not expect internal representations of first-order states to have sensory qualities representing or otherwise corresponding to such features.[15]

I did concede, in concluding the previous section, that introspection represents a first-order state under an aspect, or as being in a certain way, and this "way" doubtless has *something* to do with the first-order state's own quale or sensory quality. So if Rosenthal's term "mental quality" is taken more broadly than "sensory quality" in his original sense, it is possible that the second horn of his dilemma can be grasped, and every scanning of a first-order sensory state does "involve" some distinctive mental quality that is also distinctively related to the first-order sensory quality. I agree with Rosenthal that if one wants to maintain this, one must demystify it, but I will leave that discussion until chapter 6, especially since I have blocked the inference to his disjunctive step in the first place.

A word about the notion of an "experience": Prosecuting Rosenthal's objection against me in correspondence, Fred Dretske has asked whether unscanned perceivings or unfelt pains count as *experiences,* and whether there is an introspective "experience" involved in scanning over and above the first-order perceiving itself. To this I reply that the term "experience" is subject to the same sort of ambiguity that, in section 2 above, I ascribed to the word "feeling." One can use "experience" merely to mean a first-order perceiving or sensory state, in which case there can be unconscious experiences, or one can reserve the term for monitored sensings or monitorings of sensings, in which case "conscious experience" becomes a redundancy. I do not see any substantive issue that surpasses this verbal choice.

And a word about the relation between my inner-sense view and Rosenthal's higher-order-thought theory: Strictly, they are competitors, since I hold that awareness is a product of attention mechanisms that are perceptionlike in some ways (though not in all), and Rosenthal wants to resist this assimilation. One day I might write a paper trying to establish some advantages that my view has over his. But I do not rank that project as urgent, for in the larger context, I believe our two views are natural allies, against more demanding and more mysterious views of what conscious awareness is. We are both deflationists, holding the line against the ballooning of state/event consciousness into things it is not and need not be.

5   ESCHEWING CARTESIAN MATERIALISM

An initial flaw in the version of the inner-sense theory as stated so far is that it makes a Cartesian assumption recently highlighted by Dan Dennett (1991, chapters 5 and 6):[16] that there is some determinate stage of information-processing that constitutes the locus of conscious mental states/events. More specifically, "Cartesian materialism" is the (usually tacit) assumption that there is a *physically realized* spatial or temporal turnstile in the brain, a stage where "it all comes together" and the product of preprocessing is exhibited "to consciousness."

Dennett attacks this assumption. However natural it may be, it is gratuitous and empirically implausible: First, it is a priori unlikely that Mother Nature has furnished the human brain with any central viewing room or a single monitor to do the viewing, nor is there any positive neurophysiological sign of such an organ. Second, Dennett argues at length that the famous "temporal anomalies" of consciousness discovered by psychophysical research—such as color phi, the cutaneous rabbit, and Libet's "backward referral" of sensory experiences[17]—are anomalous only so long as Cartesian materialism is being assumed; jettison the assumption, and the phenomena are readily explained. Dennett's analyses of the experimental data are not completely uncontroversial, but I find them convincing on the whole, and it is hard to think how anyone might defend Cartesian materialism on purely neurophysiological grounds.[18]

The point is not just that there is no *immaterial audience* in the brain, nor just that there is no undischargeable homunculus, but that there is no such locus at all, however physically characterized, no single boss unit or even CPU within the brain to serve either as audience or as chief executive of my utterings and other actions. The central nervous system is as central as it gets. There is, if you like, a "stream of consciousness": "We are more-or-less serial virtual machines implemented—inefficiently—on the parallel hardware that evolution has provided for us," "Joycean" machines that formulate synthesized reports of our own passing states, though the reports are never entirely accurate (Dennett 1991, 218, 225).

The inner-sense theory has it that conscious awareness is the successful operation of an internal scanner or monitor that outputs second-order representations of first-order psychological states.[19] But an "internal scanner" sounds very much as though it presupposes an internal *audience* seated in a Cartesian theater, even if it and the theater are made of physical stuff. Then is not the inner-sense view committed to Cartesian materialism?

It is not hard to come up with a pretty damning collection of direct quotations. Armstrong spoke (above) of "*the* portion of the computing space made available for administering the *overall plan*." And (just to save you looking) I myself wrote of an internal scanner's "delivering information about . . . [a first-order] psychological state to one's *executive control unit"* (*Consciousness*, p. 72). For shame. There may be an "executive control unit" in some functional sense, but very probably not in the sense of being that agency, arrival at which makes information conscious.

But it should be clear that the inner-sense view is not per se committed to Cartesian materialism. For even if an internal scanner resembles an internal audience in some ways, the "audience" need not be seated in a Cartesian theater: There need be no *single,* executive scanner, and no one scanner or monitor need view the entire array of first-order mental states accessible to consciousness. Accordingly, there need be neither a "turnstile of consciousness" nor one central inner stage on which the contents of consciousness are displayed in one fixed temporal order. An internal monitor is an attention mechanism, which presumably can be directed upon representational subsystems and stages of same. No doubt internal monitors work selectively and piecemeal, and their operations depend on control windows and other elements of conative context. On these points, the inner-sense theory has already parted with Cartesian materialism.

A qualification: We should not throw out the baby of integration and control with the Cartesian bathwater. The operation of an internal monitor does not *eo ipso* constitute consciousness. For we can imagine a creature that has a panoply of first-order states and a rich array of monitors scanning those states, but scanning in such a way that the monitors' output contributes nothing cognitively at all to the creature's surrounding psychology, maintenance, or welfare; the outputs might just go unheard, or they might be received only by devices that do nothing but cause minute changes in the creature's skin temperature. For it to constitute consciousness, we must require that monitor output contribute specifically to the integration of information in a way conducive to making the system's behavior appropriate to its input and circumstances. Though this formulation is terribly

vague, it will do for present purposes: the present require-
ment rules out the ineffectual monitors without falling back
into the idea of a Cartesian theater or a single CPU.

(This is a good juncture at which to underscore and
deepen the teleological cast I am imparting to the inner-sense
theory. I said that for an internal monitor to count in the
analysis of consciousness, in the present sense of "conscious," the monitor must have monitoring as its function, or
one of its functions. But this is not all. To count in the analysis of *my* consciousness, the monitor must do its monitoring
for me. A monitor might have been implanted in me some-
where that sends its outputs straight to Reuters and to CNN,
so that the whole world may learn of my first-order psychological states as soon as humanly possible. Such a device teleologically would be a monitor, but it would be the wire
services' monitor rather than mine. More important, a monitor functioning within one of my subordinate homunculi
might be doing its distinctive job for that homunculus *rather
than* for me; e.g., it might be serving the homunculus's event
memory rather than my own proprietary event memory.[20]
This distinction blocks what would otherwise be obvious
counterexamples to the inner-sense view as stated so far.)

Rejection of Cartesian materialism is not only compatible with the Lockean view. In an important way it supports
the inner-sense theory: It predicts introspective fallibility of
two characteristic sorts. First, as Dennett (1991, 135–136)
emphasizes, the result of an introspective probe is a *judgment* made by the subject, which judgment does not (or not
eo ipso) simply report a "presentation" to an inner audience.
And the "temporal anomalies" alone should have made
us question the reliability of introspective reports. Introspection gets small temporal details wrong. This tends to
confirm, rather than to impugn, the inner-sense view of
consciousness. If conscious awareness is indeed a matter of
introspective attention and if introspection is the operation

of a monitor or self-scanner, then such anomalies are to be expected, for monitors and scanners are characteristically fallible on details, and Dennett (1991, chapter 6) admirably shows how such devices might corporately mix up temporal sequence in particular.

Second, if there is no single Cartesian theater, then there should be no single optimal time of probing a first-order process. More strongly, Dennett (1991, 136) argues that probing "changes the task," i.e., interferes with the very process it purports to be monitoring. This too is good news for the inner-sense theory. For if introspection is the operation of a monitor or self-scanner, then revisionary effects of the present sort are again just what we should have expected; monitoring instruments (such as ammeters) typically do affect the values of the magnitudes they measure.[21]

Thus the inner-sense theory of consciousness survives the collapse of Cartesian materialism and is even strengthened by it.

6   HILL AGAINST INNER SENSE

Christopher Hill (1991, chapter 5) offers a putative criticism of the inner-sense theory (which he calls "the inner eye hypothesis"):[22]

There has been little recognition of the fact that a sensation may be transformed by the act of coming to attend to it, and even less of the fact that a sensation may be brought into existence by attention. Instead of facing these facts and attempting to explain them, philosophers have often waged an imperialist struggle on behalf of inner vision and the inner eye hypothesis. They have maintained, either explicitly or implicitly, that inner vision is the only important form of active introspection, and they have attempted to deny or reinterpret the data that are incompatible with this view. (1991, 123–124)

When a sensation is transformed by being attended to, Hill calls this "volume adjustment"; when a sensation is brought into being by active introspection, Hill speaks of "activation." It becomes clear (Hill 1991, 126) that these two phenomena are themselves the "data" on which Hill thinks the inner-sense theory founders.

Now, what exactly is the difficulty? In particular, why cannot the inner-sense theorist grant both that scanning a first-order state can cause a change in the character of that state and that aiming one's internal monitor at a particular sector of one's phenomenal field can bring a sensation into existence? Either of these scenarios seems entirely realistic, and I, for one, do not doubt that they are sometimes realized.

In making the reply just offered, I am in effect advancing the claim that volume adjustment and activation are matters of internal scanning plus certain causal results, and perhaps Hill would object to this reductive analysis. But he uses almost overtly causal language himself: "The phenomenal field is often profoundly *changed by* the process of coming to attend to a sensation" (Hill 1991, 125; italics mine), and if he has in mind some noncausal understanding of volume control or of activation, he does not make it explicit.

A clue is provided by the following passage.

Think of a laboratory technician who is trying to determine the composition of a sample by chemical analysis. The technician may find it perfectly natural to say that he or she is "taking a closer look" at the sample. In saying this, however, the technician does not mean to assert that he or she is doing something that is fundamentally akin to what we do when we subject an object to visual scrutiny. When one subjects an object to closer visual scrutiny, one simply changes the relation between the object and one's eyes. But a technician who is analyzing a sample may well be changing many of its intrinsic qualities. (Hill 1991, 124–125)

This suggests that Hill is thinking of visual scanning as entirely passive, as unable to affect the intrinsic properties of the object scanned; analogously, he may think of "inner vision" or internal monitoring as passive in just the same

way.[23] At any rate, that would explain why he thinks the phenomena of volume adjustment and activation require different sorts of active introspection, additional to the "inner
eye" sort. But as I emphasized in the previous section, I do
not think of internal monitoring in this passive, vicarious
way; I not only grant but insist that monitoring often does
affect the phenomenal field being scanned. So if I understand
Hill's critique correctly, my own inner-sense theory is immune to it.

7 REY AGAINST INNER SENSE

On, at last, to Rey's (1983, 1988) objection. The objection is
that if all it takes to make a first-order state a conscious state
is that the state be monitored by a scanner that makes integ-
rative use of the information thus gleaned, then consciousness is a lot more prevalent than we think. Any notebook
computer, for example, has devices that keep track of its
"psychological" states. (If it be protested that no computer
has genuinely psychological states, e.g., because it has neither authentic intentional states nor sensory states, this is inessential to the point. Once we have done whatever needs to
be done to fashion a being that does have first-order intentional and sensory states, the addition of an internal monitor
or two would be virtually an afterthought, a trifling wrinkle,
surely not the sort of thing that could turn an utterly nonconscious being into a conscious being.) For that matter, individual subsystems of our own human psychologies doubtless
involve their own internal monitors, and it is implausible to
grant that these subsystems are themselves conscious.

Several replies may be made to this. First, for consciousness we should require that our monitor emit a genuine representation, not just physical "information" in the Bell
Telephone sense or just a simple nomological "indication."

But this is of little help, since surely our subsystems do contain monitors that output genuine representations.

Second, it should trouble no one that he or she has proper parts that are conscious. The proper part of you that consists of you minus your left arm is conscious, as is the part consisting of you minus your skin and most of your musculature. Other (individually) expendable chunks include your entire gastrointestinal tract, your auditory system, much of your cortex, and possibly much of a hemisphere. Each of your respective complementary proper parts is conscious, even as we speak.

But, it may be said, the second reply is of little more help than the first. For each of the large proper parts I have mentioned would qualify, mentally speaking, as being *you,* if taken on its own. Its consciousness is your consciousness, or at least there is nothing present to its consciousness that is not also present to yours. But the sort of case that worries Rey is one in which self-monitoring is performed by a *silent* subterranean subsystem, perhaps one of "all those unconscious neurotic systems postulated in so many of us by Freud, . . . [or] all those surprisingly intelligent, but still unconscious, subsystems for perception and language postulated in us by contemporary cognitive psychology" (1983, 11). What troubles Rey is that he or you or I should contain subsystems that are conscious on their own, though we know nothing of them, and whose conscious contents are not at all like ours.

It does sound eerie. But I am not so sure that the individuation of consciousnesses is so straightforward a business. For one thing, that the contents of one consciousness coextend with those of mine hardly entails that the first consciousness *is identical* with mine; they still may be two. For another, the commissurotomy literature has raised well-known thorny issues about how to count consciousnesses,[24] and these questions are made all the thornier by thought experiments such as Dan Dennett's in his classic "Where Am I?" (1978b) and more recent ones by David Sanford (1981) and Stephen White (1987). My own position is to doubt that there is any fact of the matter as to how many consciousnesses live in a single human body (or as to how many bodies can be animated by the same consciousness).

A third reply to the argument is as follows. In his own essay on Rey's objection, Stephen White (1987) enforces a distinction that Rey himself acknowledged but slighted: the difference between consciousness and *self*-consciousness. Rey (1983) had argued that if we already had a nonconscious perception-belief-desire machine, the addition of a self concept would be trifling (just as would be the addition of a simple internal monitor); one need only give the machine a first-person representation whose referent is the machine itself, i.e., add the functional analogue of the pronoun "I" to the machine's language of thought. But White argues on the basis of an ingenious group-organism example that the matter is hardly so simple and that the difference between consciousness and self-consciousness is far larger and more important than Rey allowed. Surprisingly, having a functional inner "I" does not suffice for being able to think of oneself as oneself. Nor does mere consciousness, as opposed to self-consciousness, confer personhood or any moral status. And it turns out, on White's analysis, that although subsystems of ours might count as conscious, they would not be self-conscious in the way we are. This difference helps to explain and assuage our reluctance to admit them to our own country club.[25] I find White's defense of these claims quite convincing.[26]

But I do not invest much in these second and third meditations as replies to Rey's objection (which is why I have not troubled to expound the details of White's [1987] device). I have presented them mainly for the purpose of softening you up.

So I turn to my fourth and (according to me) most important reply. It is emphatically to deny (what John Searle [1992] has recently asserted with unsurprising boldness) that consciousness is an on/off affair, that a creature is either simply conscious or simply not conscious. (If Searle did not exist, I would have to invent him, for he actually puts it that way: "Consciousness is an on/off switch; a system is either conscious or not" [Searle 1992, 83; see also McGinn 1982, 14]. I maintain that consciousness comes in degrees, which one might describe as degrees of richness or fullness.[27] We human beings are very richly conscious, but there might be more complex and/or more sophisticated organisms that are more fully conscious than we. "Higher animals" are perhaps less fully so, "lower" animals still less, and so forth.[28]

In saying this (you will have noticed), I am shifting my sense of "conscious" slightly. For there is not obviously any great spectrum of degrees of whether something has an internal monitor scanning some of its psychological states. (Actually, there probably is a *significant* spectrum, based on the extent to which monitor output contributes to integration of information and to control [as I conceded at the time, I did leave the formulation vague]. But I will not rest anything on this.) The paronymy works as follows. A thing is conscious if it is conscious to any degree at all, i.e., if it has at least one internal monitor operating and contributing etc.; we might call this *bare* or *mere consciousness*. A thing may be *more richly or more fully* conscious if it has more monitors, monitors more, integrates more, integrates better, integrates more efficiently for control purposes, and/or whatever.

Actually, I have not yet achieved paronymy, for I have located the degrees in the modifers ("richly" and "fully") rather than in the basic term "conscious" itself, which so far retains its original sense. But I do still mean to shift its meaning, for I want to allow at least a very vague sense in which some "barely" conscious devices are not really conscious; I take that to be the ordinary sense of the word. But I would insist that this sense still affords a largeish spectrum of degrees. (Granted, this needs defense, and I will provide some shortly.)

My principal answer to Rey (1983), then, is to deny his intuition: So long as it contributes in the way mentioned, one little monitor does make for a little bit of consciousness. More monitors and better integration and control make for more and fuller consciousness.[29]

As a diagnosis of his own chauvinist intuitions about machines, Rey conjectures (1983, 24) that *if* consciousness is anything, it is like an "inner light" that is on in us but could be off or missing in other creatures that were otherwise psychologically and functionally very like us at the first-order level; this is why he finds it so obvious that machines are not conscious, even when they have been hypothetically given a perception-belief-desire system like ours. (Naturally, given his conditional assumption, he asks why we should believe that *we* are not just very complicated perception-belief-desire machines, and he offers the eliminative suggestion that we are therefore not conscious either; consciousness *is not* anything.[30] But I see no reason to grant the conditional conjecture. I have no problem saying that a device whose internal monitor is contributing integration and control is conscious *of* the states reported by the monitor. There is a rhetorical difference between saying that a device is conscious *of* such and such and saying that it itself is *conscious*! But, I contend, this is *only* a rhetorical difference, barring my slight paronym above. What is special about us is not our being conscious per se but that we monitor so much at any given time and achieve so high a degree of integration and control.[31]

Thus two remarks made by psychologists and quoted by Rey as "astonishing" him by their naiveté do not astonish me in the slightest:

Perceptions, memories, anticipatory organization, a combination of these factors into learning—all imply rudimentary consciousness. (Knapp 1976, 37–69)

Depending on what Knapp meant by "anticipatory organization," this is not far wrong. If anticipatory organization implies internal monitoring that contributes, or if the "combination of . . . [the] factors into learning" involves such monitoring, or both, I endorse the statement.

Consciousness is a process in which information about multiple individual modalities of sensation and perception are combined into a unified, multidimensional representation of the state of the system and its environment and is integrated with information about memories and the needs of the organism, generating emotional reactions and programs of behavior to adjust the organism to its environment. (John 1976, 1–50)

No quarrel here either, again on the assumption that the "combining" is done in part by contributory monitoring.

The main *obstacle* to agreement with my matter-of-degree thesis is that we ourselves know only one sort of consciousness from the inside, and that one is particularly rich and full. We have elaborate and remarkably nongappy visual models of our environment; we have our other four main sense modalities, which supplement the blooming, bursting phenomenological garden already furnished by vision; we have proprioception of various sorts, which orients us within our surroundings; and (most important) we have almost complete freedom of attention within our private worlds, i.e., we can at will attend to virtually any representational aspect of any of our sensations that we choose. (All this creates the Cartesian illusion of a complete private world of sensation and thought, a seamless movie theater. There is no such completeness even phenomenologically, what with failings like the blind spot and the rapid decay of peripheral vision, but the illusion is dramatic.) Because this is the only sort of consciousness we have ever known from the inside and because the only way to *imagine* a consciousness is to imagine it from the inside, we cannot imagine a consciousness very different at all from our own, much less a greatly impoverished one. What we succeed in imagining, if we try to get inside the mind of a spider or a notebook computer, is either an implausible cartoon (with anthropomorphic talk balloons) or something that hardly seems to us to deserve the title "consciousness." It is a predicament: we are not well placed to receive the idea that there can be very low degrees of consciousness.[32]

But now, finally, for a bit of argument. (1) Consider the total mental states of people who are very ill or badly injured or suffering the effects of this or that nefarious drug. Some such people are at times called "semiconscious." Any number of altered states are possible, many of them severely diminished mental conditions. For some of these, surely, there will be no clear Searlean "Yes" or "no" to the question "Is the patient conscious?" but only a "To a degree" or "Sort of." (2) We could imagine thousands of hypothetical artifacts falling along a multidimensional spectrum having at its low end ordinary hardware-store items like record changers and air conditioners and at its high end biological human duplicates (indistinguishable from real living human beings, save by their histories).[33] Along the way(s) will be robots of many different sorts, having wildly different combinations of abilities and stupidities, oddly skewed and weighted psychologies of all kinds. Which are "conscious"? How could one possibly draw a single line separating the whole seething profusion of creatures into just two groups?

(3) For that matter, the real world provides a similar argument (for those who favor the real world over science fiction). Consider the phylogenetic scale. Nature actually contains a fairly smooth continuum of organisms, ranked roughly by complexity and degree of internal monitoring, integration, and efficient control. Where on this continuum

would God tell us that Consciousness begins? (Appropriately enough, Searle himself declares deep ignorance regarding consciousness and the phylogenetic scale.[34]) (4) If (3) does not move you (or even if (3) does), consider *human infants* as they develop from embryo to fetus to neonate to baby to child. When in that sequence does Consciousness begin?

I do not say that any of these arguments is overwhelming. But taken together—along with recognition of the imaginative predicament I mentioned prior to offering them—I believe they create a presumption. At the very least, they open the door to my matter-of-degree view and make it a contender. Therefore, one cannot simply assume that consciousness (if there is any) is an on/off switch. And Rey's argument does seem to assume this.

In conversation and correspondence, Rey has vigorously denied making this assumption. Not even his most fanciful notion of the "inner light" requires it, since the light could be on a rheostat rather than an on/off switch, so his "conditional conjecture," as I called it, is not really the issue. Certainly, he does not deny the existence of borderline cases, such as those I have mentioned above. But what, then, is his argument for denying that notebook computers, etc., are conscious to a very small degree and lie on a long continuum that has us at, or with an eye toward the future, toward, the other end? He gives none.[35]

Thus I do not think Rey has refuted the inner-sense view.

3   *The Subjectivity of the Mental*

If materialism is true, then human beings are large collections of small physical objects and nothing more, ontologically. It follows that any human being could be described, and described completely, in purely scientific terms.[1] Such a description could in principle be written out by a second human being, in the third person, and could be understood and verified by yet a third human being.

Antimaterialists and would-be materialists alike have balked at this presumptive consequence of materialism, usually on grounds having to do with the phenomenal feels of mental items. In this chapter I will focus specifically on the claim that the mental is *essentially subjective,* and for this reason cannot in fact or in principle be described in "objective" terms. Purely scientific terms are "objective"; thus, since human beings notoriously have mental attributes, materialism is false. In particular, it is often said that no materialistically acceptable third-person scientific description of a conscious human subject can capture the fact of "what it is like" *for the subject* to be in a mental state of such and such a sort. This fact, an intrinsically subjective or perspectival fact, can be known only to the subject who is in the state and to beings sufficiently similar to the subject to be able to appreciate the subject's first-person reports of what being in the state is like. Certainly nothing in physics, neurophysiology, psychology, or any other science as currently conceived can answer the question of what it is like for a bat to be having the sonar sensation (if any) associated with its vaunted echo-location technique.

As is no great secret, versions of the foregoing *knowledge argument* are presented sympathetically, if not with thorough endorsement, by Keith Gunderson (1970), Thomas Nagel (1974), and Frank Jackson (1982), among others.[2] Some can be formulated quite crisply as deductive arguments from plausible premises to the conclusion that materialism is false. I think, and argued in *Consciousness,* that none of the crisply formulable arguments comes anywhere near succeeding; all but two of them (two that do *not* trade on subjectivity[3]) are nonstarters. But there remains a feeling that "subjectivity" is an obstacle to materialism. And—I wish to admit—there remains a genuine obligation on the materialist's part to give some account of the subjectivity or perspectivalness or point-of-view aspect of the mental. That is my purpose in this chapter.

1 THREE FALLACIES

I do not know the origin, in whatever language, of the vernacular of "subjective" and "objective," except its unhelpfully obvious Latin roots in "thrown under" and "thrown against" respectively. One is tempted to assume, though for no good reason I know of, that the terms come from "subject" and "object" rather than the other way around: subjectivity has something to do with being a subject, and objectivity has something to do with being an object. But if the terms "subject" and "object" are here being used in their grammatical senses, the distinction is unrelated to the mind-body problem, for either a mental or a physical item can be a grammatical subject, and either a mental or a physical item can be a grammatical object. Even if we distinguish logical from grammatical form, the same is true for *logical* subjects and objects, on the assumption that Russell was wrong in thinking that only phenomenal objects could be genuinely named. The subjective/objective distinction as it is represented in the philosophy of mind does not seem to be a matter of reference or referents, grammatical or logical.

Lest the latter point seem to be only a preludial cough, note the apparent significance of the fact that human subjects *have* the mental properties and states in question, while other, distinct observers of the original subjects do not have them, but only look on. Looking on, physically and observationally speaking, is not the least bit like having in the first place. The bat has its sonar sensation, feeling as it does when doing its echolocation trick; the human chiropterologist who surveys the bat's neuroanatomy, however minutely, cannot have that feeling, no matter what. (And since the bat does not talk at all, much less indulge in phenomenological reporting, this means the chiropterologist can never know what it is like to have the sonar sensation.) A human being, looking at an empty but deeply cyan-colored display on a Super VGA monitor has an intense visual sensation, but a neurophysiologist monitoring that subject's brain from a good safe distance has nothing of the sort. Disparities of this kind give rise to the stereoptic (or stereoscopic) fallacy mentioned in chapter 1: We look with one eye at the brain of a human subject who is having a visual sensation. We see nothing but a gray cheesy mass, and we would see nothing else, no matter how assiduously we scraped away at the mass with our little dowel sticks (until there was nothing left). With the other eye, so to speak, we imagine *having* the intense cyan sensation. And now stereopsis fails utterly. The two eyes *will not* focus together and make a single coherent picture. The first eye's view of the subject's brain is nothing the least bit like the second eye's having the cyan sensation; the two views are totally incongruous. No third-person first-eye information about the brain or about anything else could tell us what it is like, in the second eye, to have the sensation. And this seems damning to materialism.

I hope the fallacy is plain. No materialist theory of the mind has ever entailed that *watching* the gray cheesy brain of someone who is *having* an intense cyan (or whatever) sensation is qualitatively or in any other way like having that sensation oneself. Watching the brain produces gray, cheesy visual sensations in the watcher, subserved by whatever neurophysiology underlies gray, cheesy visual sensations, and gray, cheesy sensations are, of course, *neurophysiologically* and functionally quite unlike the intense deep cyan sensations being had by the subject whose neurophysiology is being watched. No materialist has ever thought of claiming that gray, cheesy sensations are phenomenologically *or* neurophysiologically like intense deep cyan ones, and no materialist view has ever entailed or even suggested such a claim. The present (proto-)objection plays on a grammatical and/or logical subject/object distinction between a subject having *F* and a second subject regarding (as object) the first subject having *F*, which has no psychological or ontological relevance whatever.[4] Let us dismiss it, though the "intuition" it generates is hard to ignore and nags at us and makes us perseverate even after we have twigged it as a snare and a delusion.

Possibly the subjective/objective distinction is meant to be epistemic. In calling mental items "subjective," one might mean that they are *known* or presented to their owners in a way that they cannot be known to second and other parties. This too is true but also never denied by any materialist. Mental states and events are known to their hosts through introspection. Introspection, I argued in the previous chapter, is a kind of self-scanning or self-monitoring. A subject has this kind of internal access to some of his or her own first-order mental states and perhaps to a number of higher-order

49   states. But neither you nor I could have this functionally direct access to someone else's mental states (except by some futuristically special rewiring); we must either dope out the other subject's mental condition from observation of his or her neurophysiological state plus general psychophysiological knowledge or, more simply, wait to be told. I have monitors that scan my brain, you have monitors than scan yours, and so forth; that is part of what it is to be an *organism*. We do not, in nature, have scanners that directly access the brains of others. But this fact too poses no threat to materialism, since no version of materialism entails or suggests that individual organisms do have scanners that directly scan the internal operations of other organisms.

    "Subjectivity" rears its head in yet a third fallacious way: The knowledge argument tempts one to think that there is a special kind of fact, an intrinsically subjective or perspectival fact of "what it is like," that eludes physical science and "objective" science of any other sort. After all, one can know all the scientific facts about *Aplysia californica,* about bats, about human beings, about the Big Bang, about anything you like, without knowing what it is like to have any particular sensation whatever. So there is a fact left over that is inaccessible to the third-person perspective.

    Nagel and Jackson have made much of this "knowledge argument," and its premise also nags at our intuitions. But considered as argument, it will not do. Knowledge is finicky and hyperintensional: A person can know the fact that p without knowing the fact that q, even if the fact that p and the fact that q are one and the same (lightning and electrical discharge, water and H_2O). An omnivorous chemist could know all the facts there were to know about atoms and molecules but not know that what was in her glass was Perrier. The fact of its being like such and such for the bat to have its sonar sensation can be one and the same as the fact of the bat's being in a particular neurophysiological condition, even if the chiropterologist can know the latter without knowing the former. The same goes for my seeing the deep cyan display and a color-blind human neurophysiologist's failure to know what seeing cyan is like.[5]

The superficial point is clear enough, but the logic of the situation is disconcerting. One would think that Leibniz's Law would hold here: if $F_1 = F_2$, then if F_1 is known to someone S, F_2 is known to S. That principle demonstrably does not hold here or anywhere, but one is hard put to say just why not. I will argue in section 3 below that (not surprisingly) knowledge involves the mode under which the knower represents the fact known and that this is no less true for mental facts than for ordinary physical ones.

There is also a question of whether there *could be* intrinsically perspectival facts of the sort that seem to be "left over" once all the third-person, scientific facts are set aside. A simple argument reveals the prima facie problem:[6] To every fact there corresponds a true proposition (I fall into the vernacular of "propositions," allowing that it may be only heuristic or fictional). A proposition is a composite made of concepts: individual concepts and predicative concepts. Each concept or Fregean intension can be represented in the standard way as a function from possible worlds to extensions. Thus to every proposition there corresponds a set of possible worlds, structured by functions from worlds to individuals and sets of individuals. And any such structured set can be described (or could be described by an omniscient intelligence) in "objective," third-person terms if we had enough names and predicates to go around. The original fact, even if it is a fact of "what it is like" to be in some mental state, could then be described by reference to the structured set of worlds and is not intrinsically perspectival after all, QED. Here again, the result is counterintuitive, for how can an initial apparent inscrutability be made pellucid by some mumbo jumbo about functions from "possible worlds" to whatever? But here again, if the argument does not work, it will be instructive to see why not.[7]

2 THE BANANA PEEL

There is still a fourth issue to get out of the way, occasioned by some later passages of Nagel's (1974) article. For example, on p. 444 he talks of taking a "subjective *viewpoint toward* our experience" [my italics], and on p. 448 he talks of "how [his experiences] *appear to*" him [also my italics]. He is thinking of experience and experiences as *things* that appear to us, things toward which we "take viewpoints." From here it is a natural leap to the conclusion that since no one else can take the *same* viewpoint toward my experiences that I do (again, probably because no one else has them), my experiences "appear to" me in a unique way, and the fact of their doing so is inaccessible to description by any third party.

Note Nagel's striking slip into "act-object" jargon. In speaking of experiences as things that present appearances to us and toward which we take viewpoints, he makes them into objects of consciousness, as if we *encountered* them from time to time. No wonder, then, that their "owners" should stand in a *special* proprietary relation to them and that such a state of affairs should have a special ontological status. But there are three things wrong here.

First and least, Nagel's act-object formulation begs the question against the materialist, or would beg the question if incorporated into the premises of an antimaterialist argument. For no materialist I know of has ever granted the existence of purely mental objects scanned by a third eye of the mind. Modern materialists reject sense data, afterimages, pains, and the like, qua phenomenal individuals; instead they offer adverbial and/or "topic-neutral" deflationary analyses of attributions that seem to quantify over such things. It is not sensations considered *as objects* of mental acts that the materialist (token-)identifies with physical events, but only sensations, in the sense of sens*ings* and events of experienc*ing*. The inadvertent neglect of this fact, typically on the part of theorists who demonstrably know better, was what in *Consciousness* I called "the Banana Peel."[8] (Notice that this is a criticism not of Nagel's main argument but only of what I consider a small side issue in his article; I have brought it up only as a cautionary tale.) Thus the materialist need not listen to premises couched in act-object form, unless the venue of debate is shifted to the question per se of phenomenal objects versus adverbial and topic-neutralist attempts to eliminate them.

A bold move is suggested by this last clause. Suppose that someone who hears the present charge of question-begging is thereby goaded out of the closet. That is, suppose an antimaterialist, having spent enough time in the closet to observe that the Emperor has no clothes, says forthrightly that there *damn well are* phenomenal individuals such as sense data—afterimages and so forth—that we damn well are acquainted with them, that "adverbialism" and topic-neutralism are just so much posturing, without substance, and that not just naive intuitions but powerful arguments can be urged in their favor. (Frank Jackson [1977] has done just this.) Someone who makes this move avoids the initial charge of question-begging by seriously joining the debate over phenomenal objects and defending them against their detractors. I personally think this to be the single most powerful and damaging antimaterialist strategy that exists anywhere.[9] (It is the main topic of the next chapter.) But it leads straight to the second of our three difficulties for Nagel's act-object formulation: If the antimaterialist comes out of the closet in the way suggested, then (a) no further *argument against materialism* is needed. For if there really are phenomenal individuals, it follows *immediately* that materialism is false: phenomenal individuals are in no sense physical objects, and if human sensory states are relations between human subjects and phenomenal objects, then human sensory states cannot be described entirely in physical terms.[10] Thus the mundane materialist/antimaterialist debate becomes superfluous. Moreover, (b) if the existence of phenomenal individuals is what is at issue, subjectivity as such drops out of the picture. "Subjectivity," "perspective," "viewpoint" are vague and unimportant notions compared to the actual existence of nonphysical individual things. Of course, the nonphysical individuals could be expected to have some (other) strange properties, such as that of appearing to only one person at a time, and subjectivity may be presumed to fall pretty trivially out of those.

The third drawback to Nagel's act-object usage is that it misrepresents the *locus* of subjectivity. Nagel talks of being appeared to by, and taking viewpoints toward, our experiences. But if "experiences" are not after all objects, phenomenal individuals, they are adverbially qualified or taxonomized events. They are appear*ings* and viewpoint-tak*ings*, whose objects are real or fancied elements of the external world. Of course, we represent the external world in any number of ways, and any such representation is a representation from a point of view; this point-of-view aspect remains to be accounted for. But it hardly follows that an event of representing or viewpoint-taking on someone's part cannot itself be represented by someone else in a third-person, scientific way. A simple machine model would help here: one machine can scan or survey an item from its own point of view (determined by its "sensory" limitations and its spatial location with respect to the item), while another machine can scan the first machine, its internal states, the item in question, and the scanning relation obtaining between the two.

All or most of us would like to think, in our scientistic way, that psychologists and brain physiologists are moving toward better and better objective descriptions of mental facts. Nagel deplores this wishful thought as quixotic; he thinks that mental facts are intrinsically subjective and so in principle can never be "objectively" described by any science. To offer a description purporting to be "objective" would be, he says, to take the subjectivity out of the experience and so to fail to describe that experience as it is or was. But here Nagel is misled by his inadvertent act-object model. To describe a subject's experienc*ing* from an external, third-person point of view is not to wrench the subjectivity out of the experiencing and replace it with a distorted or distorting objectivity but rather is to push toward a better description of the experiencing as a whole, subjectivity and all. The subjectivity is immanent to the experiental event, but this does not prevent us from describing the whole event objectively.

3 SUBJECTIVITY AS PRONOMINAL

I take all the foregoing to show that no one has yet come up with a convincing or even plausible antimaterialist argument based on subjectivity per se. I have also offered a bit of diagnosis of the temptation to think (falsely) that such an argument exists. But as yet I have provided no positive account of subjectivity, and I grant that the materialist owes the world an explanation of what it is about a mental/neural state that makes its proprietor think of it as subjective and intrinsically perspectival.

As I have hinted, some of the explanation is supplied by the fact that our perceptual processors are *filters;* they take in and retain only a tiny and tendentiously selected fraction of the information available in an object under scrutiny. When real human beings regard a physical object from different visual points of view, they take in different and all highly selective bunches of information about that object. When they apply different sensory modes to the object, the disparity and the incompleteness of the respective bunches of information become far more dramatic, as in the story of the blind men and the elephant.[11] *Part* of the way in which our perceptual experience of an object is subjective is this: On any occasion in real life, no two subjects perceive the same physical object in the same way; no two subjects obtain and record just the same information about the object. Accordingly, their files on the object differ, and differ in a way that affects behavior. Thus upon perceiving the object, they are affected differently and their "functional profiles" change in nonparallel ways, even when we allow for the fact that the functional profiles were not the same to begin with. So from the plain, bare initial fact that sense-organs are filters, we may infer two things that are obvious sources of "subjectivity" intuitions: Different subjects differ informationally with respect to the same external environment, and they differ functionally in that they acquire different second-order dispositions with respect to the same external environment. Perhaps this is subjectivity enough.

Yet more can be said. As I have observed here and there, Nagel's argument seems closely connected to the older issue, raised by Geach (1957) and Castañeda (1966), of the alleged irreducibility of self-regarding propositional attitudes and the alleged intrinsic perspectivalness of self-regarding beliefs, such as my own belief that *I myself* am undereducated and my colleague's belief that *he himself* is undereducated.[12] This issue too features "perspectival facts" in some form, since the belief contents in question cannot be rendered in any third-person way. If someone else were to opine of me, "W.G.L. is undereducated," this would not express the same thought as my own, for if I were amnesic, I might share this opinion without having the very thought that *I myself,* as opposed to that person W.G.L., is undereducated. The point is nowadays tediously familiar. But it can be turned aside or at least rendered unsurprising and ontologically harmless.[13] The way in which this is done is cognate with the way in which the knowledge argument is defused and *also* with what I think is the ultimate explication of subjectivity.

Beliefs (I assume) are inner representational states of subjects' nervous systems.[14] As such, they have properties of two distinctive sorts: They have truth conditions, representable either as general or singular propositions or as sets of possible worlds, and they have functional and/or computational and/or inferential roles in their hosts' behavioral economies. Beliefs' constituent concepts, both general and individual, share this dual nature. A concept has both an extension—a set of items to which it applies—and a functional profile within its owner's psychology, which helps both to guide the owner's behavior, given a total set of stimuli, and to determine the extension of the concept, given ambient environmental and social factors. (Thus the concepts "water" and "H_2O" have the same extension but distinct functional profiles in most people; the concepts "my left foot" as used by me and by President Clinton have similar functional profiles but radically different extensions.) The lesson I draw from the late 1970s literature on "methodological solipsism" (Putnam 1975, Fodor 1980, Stich 1978a, Burge 1979) is that a concept's functional role and the same concept's extension are strictly independent of each other *and* far less conditioned by each other than one would unreflectively think; this is shown both by Twin-Earth-style examples and by multifarious indexical cases. Concepts that are functionally very different may coextend *even throughout logical space* (think of mathematical concepts), and concepts that are functionally just alike—even shared by all molecular duplicates—may differ in extension (though normally a functional role *together with a context* will determine an extension).

CHAPTER THREE

What is special about representations "*de se*" is just that they have both a distinctive functional role *and* a distinctive extensional feature *that nowhere else coincide*. Crucially, a concept is counted as a *self* concept or mental "*I*" only if (1) it functions inferentially and otherwise computationally as an "I," (2) it has its owner as the sole member of its extension, *and* (3) no one else could use a computationally parallel concept of their own to designate the original owner. (Compare the use of "I" in English: it has a distinctive inferential role, it has its utterer, say W.G.L., as the sole member of its extension, and no one else can use the word "I" to designate W.G.L.)

Yagisawa (1987) has claimed that the mode of presentation involved in a *de se* ascribed belief of mine *necessarily* both presents me (W.G.L.) as its object and "*a fortiori . . .* necessarily presents something [actually existent] to me in every context"; a merely *de re* mode having me as its extension does not have either of these properties essentially. That, says Yagisawa, is how any "merely reflexively *de re*" belief-ascription differs from a genuinely *de se* ascription: the latter somehow captures the fact that the mode of presentation involved in the reported belief has the modal properties just mentioned. "*De se* ascriptions are (indexically) *de dicto* ascriptions which are automatically *de re* ascriptions such that the *res* is the believer" (Yagisawa 1987, 180).

I grant Yagisawa's claim—in one sense that I will elaborate below, and waiving quibbles about his notion of necessity *de re*. What I deny is only (a) that the dual feature is unique in kind and (b) that the feature has any ontological import whatever.

As regards (a), note that other attitude ascriptions have comparable *kinds* of distinctive dual features, even if they do not share that one. Yagisawa's special mode of presentation must be individuated very narrowly, according to its referent *as well as* its independent and also distinctive functional or computational role, since otherwise—if it were picked out by computational role alone or by referent alone—it would either fail to apply *necessarily* to the referent or fail to be distinctively first-person, respectively. I have no quarrel with this very fine-grained way (or any other way) of individuating modes of presentation. But if we are allowed simultaneously to place both computational and referential requirements on modes of presentation, we can exhibit any number of other belief ascriptions that appear to differ from the "merely *de re*." Steven Boër and I have given any number of examples in previous works (1980, 462–463; 1987): the *de verbo,* involving quote names (we could not properly assert "John believes that 'Cicero' is an adjective" unless John himself represented the word "Cicero" by means of its quote name and thereby successfully designated the word "Cicero"); the *de numero* ("John believes that 9 is the number of the planets" cannot strictly be paraphrased by "John believes that *t* numbers the planets" for any term *t* that either has a different psychological role from the numeral "9" or designates something other than the number 9); the special term "dthis" (which by definition designates itself on any occasion of its utterance).[15]

As regards (b), observe carefully that the conceded distinctiveness of the self concept has no metaphysical fallout of any sort that would encourage partisans of Cartesian egos, Butlerian selves, Nagelian perspectival facts, or the like. Certainly it reveals no ontological specialness of the self. It is merely the circumstantial joint result of the functional and extensional roles of "I" in speech and in the language of thought, and derivatively of the reportive use of (admittedly distinctive) reflexive pronouns that reflect that tandem feature. I will expand on this point in section 5.

Here is the connection with the failure of the "knowledge argument." Knowledge of any fact is knowledge under a representation. One and the same fact may be known or unknown to a subject, depending on that subject's mode of representing that fact; e.g., knowledge of the fact that a glass of water is being thrown in one's face by an enraged party guest is not, *eo ipso*, knowledge that H_2O is being thrown in one's face. Modes of representation individuate far more finely than extensions, even when "extensions" are taken to be full-blown states of affairs rather than just 'tuples of objects. (Extensions can also individuate more finely than functional roles, as the Twin-Earth and indexical examples show, though this does not affect the knowledge argument.) This is why, in general, one may not know a fact F_1 even though one knows F_2 and $F_1 = F_2$. The difference is not semantic, but rather lies in the functional role of representations. In particular, "water" has an *inferential* role quite distinct from that of "H_2O." And so does knowledge that one is having this sort of sensation and knowledge that one is in brain state such and such, even though one's having this sort of sensation is just one's being in brain state such and such. (One might, of course, insist on a notion of facts or states of affairs that incorporated the mode of presentation, in such a way that such items did obey Leibniz's Law as regards being known. But in this fine-grained sense, the fact of water being thrown would not be the fact of H_2O's being thrown, yet no one would on this account become a dualist or a vitalist about water.)

McGinn makes a closely related point: "A difference of representation does not imply a genuine disagreement. . . . Two people in different places do not disagree if one calls 'here' what the other describes as 'there'; there would be disagreement only if they *both* referred to the same place as 'here'" (1983, 21). Similarly, one can know that something is happening *here,* and not know that that thing is happening *there,* even if "here" and "there" turn out to be one and the same place.

A human being's internal monitors give representations as their output, second-order representations of the subject's own first-order psychological states. If a subject *S* hosts such a representation, no one else can use a syntactically similar representation to represent the very first-order state token (of S's own) that is the object of S's own representation. Other people may be able to form syntactically similar representations, but the objects of those representations will be first-order states of their own hosts, not any states of S's. (Think of the public English phrase "my right elbow": people other than S can use other singular terms to designate S's right elbow, and people other than S can use the very same term "my right elbow" to designate their own right elbows, but only S can use that term to designate S's right elbow.) It does not follow that such representations cannot be used to type-classify other subjects' first-order mental states or right elbows. Rather, it follows only that the self-ascriptive combination of syntactic type and referent is invariably unique.

The foregoing notion of syntactic similarity could use some spelling out. Think of a representation as a token in the subject's language of thought. (I believe that representations actually are tokens in their owners' languages of thought, but if you disagree, just make the supposition for heuristic purposes.[16] As an immediate consequence of the operation of one of S's internal scanners, S tokens a mental word for the type of first-order state being scanned. This word would not be lexically composite; its meaning would not be the compositional result of a semantic compounding operation performed on the prior meanings of its morphologically proper parts. It would be semantically primitive. And since its inferential and/or conceptual role would be unique to its subject in the way I have described, it would certainly not be synonymous with any primitive or composite expression of public English. In this sense it would be a private name as well as semantically primitive, a name that only its actual user could use to name its actual referent.[17]

Incidentally, the point exposes a further source of "bat" disquiet: Insofar as we think of the bat as being conscious or as having a *feely* sonar sensation at all, we may naturally suppose the bat to have conceptual resources alien to us and in particular to apply a concept to the sensation that is not even potentially available to humans. Thus the bat thinks something that we cannot and never could understand. It seems to follow that there is something to understand, something that outruns all the scientific and other third-person facts that we and our chiropterologists do understand.[18]

If our human introspective concepts are semantically primitive lexemes of our languages of thought and if we do think of the bat as mobilizing concepts at all, then it is only fair to grant that the bat's concept of the sonar sensation is likewise a semantically primitive lexeme of its language of thought. And certainly this mental word will be synonymous with neither any public word of English nor any word of any human being's language of thought.[19] Thus, just as I can refer to my pain using a concept that no one else can use to refer to my pain, the bat can refer to its sonar sensation using a concept that no human could use at all. But as before, it does not follow that the bat knows or understands a *different fact,* unless in an especially fine-grained sense of "fact" that in no way embarrasses materialism. The bat "understands something that we cannot" only in the same sense as that in which the chemist knows something that a chemical illiterate cannot when both see water splashing from a thrown glass.[20]

Lewis (1990) considers something like the move I have made here based on a "language of thought" hypothesis, but he rejects it. He grants a thin sense in which, by gaining new words and storing new sentences, a person can acquire new "information" even though no metaphysical possibilities are eliminated. But on this view, "the special role of experience turns out to be on a par with the special role of Russian. If the language of thought picks up new words by borrowing from public language, then lessons in Russian add new words, and result in the storing of new sentences, and thereby impart 'information' that never could have been had from lessons in English" (Lewis 1990, 510).

So far as this objection is addressed to my view, it misses the point. First, as Van Gulick (1992) points out, the difference between Russian and English synonyms is hardly so great as that between two functionally different modes of presentation having the same referent (such as "the mother of my child" and "the founding director of Women's Voices of Chapel Hill"), much less so great as that between a human scientist's description of a bat's sonar state and the bat's biological means (if any) of registering that same state. (See Gilman 1994 on the vast functional differences between perceptual representations and linguistic representations of the same thing.)

Second, Lewis ignores the essential indexicality. What makes subjective knowledge intrinsically perspectival is that it is pronominal. Intrinsically perspectival experiences are uncannily like intrinsically perspectival self-regarding beliefs, and Lewis's analogy misses that entirely.

4 AN EPISTEMIC OBJECTION AND THE EXPLANATORY GAP

The foregoing general point about the semantic primitiveness of introspective mental words enables us to counter a further objection to materialism, first formulated by Levine (1983). The complaint is roughly that the philosophical evidence for the token identity of mental states with neurophysiological states is too indirect and is not analogous to the epistemic handles we have on other a posteriori identities. Consider clouds and masses of water droplets. As Place (1956) conceded, one can establish the identity directly and perceptually by going up in a balloon and rising continuously into a cloud one is watching. In the case of the Morning Star and the Evening Star, a sophisticated astronomy can simply track the planet Venus using reliable instruments and establish both that *and why* it appears as Hesperus at morning and as Phosphorus at evening. In the case of lightning and electrical discharge, the identification explains why lightning appears as a flash and emits a crackling boom, for we already know that everyday electrical discharges spark and crackle on a proportionately smaller scale. In the case of genes and DNA segments, we see on the basis of the double-helix structure why Mendelian combinatorics are as they are. In the case of water and H_2O, the known microproperties of hydrogen and oxygen molecules explain why water is clear (it does not filter light) and why it is liquid (the molecules slip readily past each other). But we have no such explanation in the case of sensations and brain processes. We are told that the token-identity thesis avoids the awfulness of dualism, avoids the crudeness and implausibility of meataxe behaviorism, explains mind-brain correlations, falls naturally out of the causal analysis of the mental, squares with empirically tutored modal intuitions, etc. But these philosophical virtues are diffuse and characteristically speculative. The token-identity thesis does nothing to *trace* the relation of sensations to neural firings, and it does nothing to explain why sensations have the particular feels they do, even given its philosophical tenability. In these senses, materialism has failed to *account for* consciousness, even if there is no formal incompatibility between materialism and any fact of consciousness and even if materialism is supported by abstract philosophical argument. There is, as Levine says, an explanatory gap.[21]

I am not at all sure that this disanalogy should by itself make us discount the abstract philosophical argument, even if we grant that our total evidence for the identity thesis is weaker than our evidence for any of the other a posteriori identifications; the philosophical considerations are still powerful, absent any palpably convincing objection to the mind-brain identification per se. But our internal-monitoring model supplemented by our language-of-thought metaphor provide a more positive response to the explanatory-gap objection: the lack of tracings and explanations of the sort demanded is *just what you would expect* if the self-scanner view of introspection is correct.

My mental reference to a first-order psychological state of my own is a tokening of a semantically primitive Mentalese lexeme. My mental word is functionally nothing like any of the complex expressions of English that in fact refer to the same (neural) state of affairs; certainly it is neither synonymous with, nor otherwise semantically related to, any of them. And since no one else can use that mental word or even any functionally and syntactically similar word of their own to designate that state of affairs, of course no one can explain in English or in any other language why that state of affairs feels like [*that* or *semantha*] to me. Introspection involves a very special mode of presentation, primitive and private in the senses I have described. This is why the tracings and explanations are not forthcoming, despite the more general body of philosophical motivation.[22] Therefore, the lack of such tracings and explanations, only to be expected, do not count against the materialist identification. They almost count in its favor.

Two analogies may help to make the point against the explanatory-gap objection. First, consider a person K.'s aesthetic response to certain paintings. These paintings all seem to K. to have something in common. K. cannot put any literal English word(s) on what the paintings have in common; *faute de mieux,* he calls it "blutsiness."[23] He can say nothing about blutsiness save that he knows it when he sees it. And in fact his blutsiness judgments are reliable and repeatable: confronted with a painting he called blutsy eleven years ago but has not seen since and has forgotten, he will call it blutsy again. Now a local art critic who is also a perceptual psychologist makes a study of K. and the paintings K. has seen, and by a combination of great skill and great good luck she manages to isolate an artistic property—an unbelievably complex pattern of colors, light-shade relations, impasto, and so on—of the "blutsy" paintings that uniformly causes K. to ascribe blutsiness. On excellent evidence, she hypothesizes that what K. calls "blutsiness" is just this complex artistic property. And this hypothesis is entirely reasonable. But it does not explain why paintings having the complex property look *blutsy* to K. It cannot explain this. Nothing can. No amount of technical palaver about saturations and texture gradients and so forth would seem *to K.* to have anything to do with blutsiness, for "blutsy" is his private and perspectival word for the physical property as it distinctively manifests itself to him.[24] But these facts *in no way* embarrass the art-critic-cum-psychologist's hypothesis.

The second analogy (already suggested in the previous section): If I am amnesic or the like, I can have any amount of factual information, even *de re* information, about *W.G.L.* without having that information about myself. The information may seem to me totally irrelevant, a biography of someone I have never known and care nothing about (some academic philosopher in America who does not even ski); I read a biography of W.G.L. unmoved. Here the connection may seem "traceable": my wife's lawyer might assemble all sorts of physical evidence to show that I, in my present amnesic identity, am one and the same person as W.G.L. But the evidence would all be third-person-descriptive. "I" would be identified by the lawyer as *the person who is F, G, . . . ,* and it would still be left to me to judge that *I* am that person. If I

am sufficiently amnesic, I may not so judge. Neither the lawyer nor anyone else can *explain why* W.G.L., or why the person who is *F, G,* . . . , is *me*. Yet these persons are in fact both
me, and we can have excellent reason to believe that.[25]

5 SUBJECTIVITY AGAIN

Finally I turn to the subjectivity of sensation. Sensory experience represents.[26] And a representation corresponds to a *selective set of properties*. This is because of the perspectival,
filtering feature noted in section 3 above, and it is also why
philosophical items like Frege's senses, Russell's descriptions, Meinong's objects, and Castañeda's "guises" have
been so attractive. Unsurprisingly, different representations
differ functionally or computationally from each other even
when they are representations of the same thing and have exactly the same *semantics*, in the truth-conditional sense.

As we have seen, though self-regarding attitudes differ
functionally from other attitudes directed upon the very
same state of affairs, they have just the same truth condition,
that state of affairs itself. There is no extra fact that is known,
believed, or whatever. I know that *I myself* weigh 180
pounds, while you know only that W.G.L.—as you represent
him—weighs 180 pounds, but it is the same fact that we
both know.

To "know what it is like" to have such and such a sensation is likewise a functional rather than a referential matter,
on the assumption that there is no logically private reference
to the quale of an immaterial sense datum (see section 2
above).[27] To sense or to feel is to sense something under a representation. If you allude to the firing of my c fibers while I
complain of pain, we refer to the very same state of affairs.
But our respective functional states that happen to result in
our doing so are quite different. And the functional state

of the bat having its sonar sensation is *of course* entirely different from that of the chiropterologist examining the bat's neurophysiology. Nonetheless, one and the same fact is apprehended by both (so far as the bat does "apprehend" its own sensations).

Here again the explanation is simple. I know my pain by introspection, and my representation of disorder is directly formed by introspection and has obvious immediate inferential and other functional properties. The bat's sonar sensation too has its immediate functional causes and effects as a direct consequence of the bat's internal monitoring and effector system. No one else—human, bat, or bat-human—could know the same facts *by being in the same functional state*.[28] This last fact is, if anything is, the subjectivity of the mental.

And the fact quite naturally creates the illusion of an ontologically special kind of state of affairs. After all, we are in our heads with ourselves, and our own psychological states' functional doings are of paramount importance; small wonder that introspective hints of these roles should color our first-order perceptions of external objects. Indeed, when one puts it this way, it is almost analytic that the illusion should be generated. The inner mode of presentation determined by a representation's functional role has little relation to the object that is the representation's extension, and as we have seen, the *pair* consisting of the functional role and the extension is unique to the subject: anyone else might be in a state having the same functional role, and anyone else might be in a state having the same extension, but no one else can be in a state having both—just as anyone besides me can use the word "I" to designate themselves, and anyone else can use some word to designate me, but no one else can do both (only I can use "I" to designate W.G.L.). Sensing this, we think there must be something very special about ourselves, our *selves*.

Human and other subjects can have functionally or computationally different states that nonetheless home in on the same objective state of affairs, either external or internal. But there are no intrinsically subjective or perspectival facts that are either the special objects of self-regarding attitudes or facts of "what it is like." There are only states of subjects that both function in a particularly intimate way within those subjects and have the subjects themselves and their other states as inevitable referents. And this, I think, is all there is to subjectivity.[29]

Qualia Strictly So Called

My purpose in this chapter is to commit a fallacy—or rather, to continue defending a position that has been *labeled* a fallacy, by Ned Block, who ("tendentiously") calls it "the fallacy of intentionalizing qualia" (1990, 55).

As I declared in chapter 1, my larger project is to secure the hegemony of representation, the doctrine that the mental and the functional/intentional are one and the same and that the mind has no distinctive properties that outrun its functional and intentional properties. The hegemony of representation, specifically applied to qualia, is precisely Block's "fallacy of intentionalizing qualia." In my view, Block has committed the "*fallacy* fallacy," that of imputing fallaciousness to a view with which one disagrees but without doing anything to show that the view rests on any error of reasoning (compare "the naturalistic fallacy," etc.). I will return to Block's fallacy in chapter 6.

Take phenomenal color as a paradigm case of a quale, and let us be unusually careful about our use of this unhappy word. The sense I have in mind is roughly C. I. Lewis's (1929) original sense, in which a *quale* is the introspectible monadic qualitative property of what seems to be a phenomenal individual, such as the color of what Russell called a visual sense datum.[1] For example, if S is visually healthy and looking at a ripe tomato in good light, the tomato will look red to S, and if S focuses her introspective attention on the corresponding subregion of her visual field, S will see that subregion as an individual red patch having a roundish shape. The redness of that phenomenal patch is the quale of the containing visual sensation.[2] One registers such a quale whenever one perceives a colored object as such.

I think it is very important to resist the sloppy use of the "q" word (invariably in the unwitting plural, like "data" or "media") as a sort of generic or umbrella term for matters of consciousness, subjectivity, phenomenal character, etc. This neologism—apart from its being a neologism in the first place and a sense-diluting one at that—just reinforces the tendency, deplored in chapter 1, to lump many different phenomena, problems, and issues indiscriminately together. We should be vigorously doing the opposite, taking care to use our terms more precisely and finickingly, in order to make some progress at least by ceasing to talk past each other, as now we do constantly.[3]

As per the hegemony of representation, I would like to explain the whole matter of color and the other secondary qualities exclusively in terms of ordinary natural science plus plausible claims about functional organization and mental representation. In chapter 8 of *Consciousness* I made what I consider to be a strong beginning; here I will again expound the view I have been developing, confront a very nasty problem having to do with inverted spectra, and then answer an astute objection made by Kobes (1991).

1 THE THEORY OF PHENOMENAL COLOR

What are we to make of color qualia, the apparently first-order properties of apparent phenomenal individuals? (This is the problem ebulliently labeled (H) in chapter 1 above.)

As materialists rather than phenomenalists, we hate the idea of acknowledging Russellian sense data as actual constituents of the real world. Since the 1950s, the standard move against sense data has been to "go adverbial" and speak of sensing redly or mauvely, rather than of being acquainted with a red or mauve thing. But for reasons similar to Frank Jackson's (1977), I think that adverbialism is hopeless as a refuge from reference to phenomenal individuals. Adverbializing does not in fact remove the apparatus of quantification over such things, for the adverbial constructions in question are not semantically primitive but have a structure that is revealed by the patterns of entailment relations holding between the sentences in which they figure, and (as I argued in *Consciousness*) this structure involves just the same sorts of quantification and term reference that the adverbial theory was designed to eschew. Apparent singular reference to phenomenal individuals, such as pointy light-green spots in one's visual field, remains to be accounted for, and the obvious explanation is that the apparent singular reference is genuine.

But, thankfully, we need not admit sense data. For in the tradition of Anscombe (1965), Hintikka (1969), Thomason (1973), Adams (1975, 1991), Kraut (1982), and Lewis (1983a), we can treat phenomenal individuals as *intentional inexistents*. Suppose Bertie experiences a pointy green afterimage. There is a green spot in his visual field; if he denies it, he is a liar. He may sincerely believe that he is sensing and confronted by something green and pointy, but (we may suppose) there is no physical green thing in Bertie's line of sight, and certainly there is no green thing in his brain. It merely *seems* to Bertie that there is a pointy green individual before him; it is visually in his mind as if a pointy green object were before him. And this impression of his is simply mistaken. The psychophysiologist can explain the illusion, for Bertie's visual analyzers are functioning in some of the same ways in which they do when Bertie is really confronted by a green physical object.

In my view, the best going semantics for intentional inexistence is a possible-worlds semantics: The apparent mental references to phenomenal individuals are really to objects existing in or "at" alternative worlds. I maintain that the latter otherworldly objects are physical at their containing worlds, so we need not worry anywhere about *nonphysical* phenomenal individuals.[4] Granted, we need to explain the physical natures of their qualitative properties in their own containing worlds. (But it is important to see that the possible-worlds metaphysics is inessential to my more fundamental claim that apparent sense data are intentional objects. I happen to think that intentional inexistents are denizens of other possible worlds—or in some cases impossible worlds—but if you have a different metaphysic of intentional inexistents, apply it forthwith, and do not waste paper criticizing mine. Have a nice day.)

For that matter, we need to explain the physical natures of objects' color properties in our own real world. My scheme makes phenomenal color parasitic on the real colors of physical objects. It has been more popular throughout history to work in the other direction, to explain the colors or alleged colors of physical objects in terms of the colors attaching to visual sensations, and for good reason, since "real physical" color has proved elusive. The natural sciences have pathetically failed to provide any decent correlates of what we human beings take to be the real, stable colors of physical objects.[5]

What is a would-be color realist to do? I buy into David Armstrong's view of physical color,[6] taken up more recently by David Rosenthal (1990a, 1991a) and Dan Dennett (1991, 375–383) also.[7] It construes physical colors as physical properties of objects, but only as very modest ones; it does not flatter those properties in any way. They are roughly the properties that would, indeed do, constitute their owners' dispositions to produce the corresponding sensations in sentient observers under normal viewing conditions, and as we know, these properties are an unruly, rough, and ragged lot.[8] Almost certainly they form no natural kind.

A physical color, then, probably is a woefully disjunctive microstructural property of objects and is scientifically quite ill behaved. It is surely no "genuine universal," and, more to the point, it is of interest only because of its relation to the human visual system.

The latter fact has led philosophers to overlook Armstrong's option. For the following argument seems very powerful: "(1) You (admit that you) pick out the 'property' in question only by reference to the human visual system. And in fact, (2) all that 'its' instances have in common is that they do produce the relevant sensations in people. Moreover, (3) you have admitted the property constitutes its subject's disposition to produce such sensations. For each of these reasons—and certainly following from their conjunction—the property you're talking about is just that of *being disposed to cause people to sense* in the corresponding way. So you've failed to break out of the circle." We had been trying to explicate "phenomenal color" in terms of real color, but now we are tacitly understanding "real color" in terms of the phenomenal; bah.

But it is not so, and the argument I have just stated is, however seductive, a bad one. Admittedly, the kind of property we are talking about is ontologically and scientifically ugly, but neither any of the premises (1) through (3) individually nor even their conjunction justifies the argument's conclusion. Despite its ugliness, my sort of property inheres in an object on its own, regardless of how it is picked out or identified by me or anyone else, regardless of its ever producing sensations in anyone (or being detected by any being at all), and surprisingly, regardless of its actually constituting a disposition to produce sensations in anything. For in principle, it can be specified or defined independently of its doing any of these things. It is as it is, whether or not anyone identifies it or refers to it, whether or not it ever produces sensations of any sort, whether or not it constitutes any disposition, and even if none of these were true.

Of course, color realism faces a number of other objections, and confronting them would require too large a digression in a book on philosophy of mind. (I have begun this project in Lycan, in preparation, b.) But two of the problems deserve at least a bit further mention here. First, what are "normal viewing conditions," if not just, circularly, the conditions in which a colored object produces the corresponding sensation in viewers? Here I turn to the work of Roger Shepard (1990, 1991, 1992), who offers an independent characterization of "normal viewing conditions" in evolutionary/ecological terms. The idea is roughly that normal conditions are those that prevailed on the earth's surface throughout the eons during which color constancy was established in our ancestors, but this is a longish story.

Second, as Georges Rey has asked me, is there not still a vicious circularity in the way in which my Armstrongian color properties are to be identified, i.e., in what is supposed to determine the properties' disjuncts? Briefly, my idea is to take as given (1) standard human visual physiology, (2) normal viewing conditions understood in Shepard's way or something like it, and (3) subjects' verbal judgments about the colors of objects. Together, these three factors should in principle yield a reference-fixing triangulation of any given Armstrongian color property.

For the sake of argument, then, I will assume some such version of color realism. Now, how does phenomenal color depend upon real color? My answer is, by representation: for a visual state to have or contain or feature a green quale in my strict sense is for it to represent greenness—real physical greenness—at some location in the visual field. What, in turn, is it for a brain state or event to represent greenness?

CHAPTER FOUR

That depends on one's psychosemantics, as Jerry Fodor calls it, i.e., one's general view of how any mental/brain state or event represents anything.

I myself have no worked-out psychosemantics to plug in. My sympathies lie with etiological accounts of representation, and mc⁻e specifically with teleologized etiological accounts (Van Gulick 1980; Richardson 1981; Millikan 1984, 1989; Dretske 1988), but I cannot defend or even survey these attempts here. In lieu of such a defense, I will adopt a placeholder sort of view and say, *for the sake of discussion,* that an apparent visual object is phenomenally green, and its containing sensation is "of green" or represents greenness, iff this sort of sensation is "normally caused by" green physical objects. An organism senses greenly iff it is in the sort of state distinctively brought on by visual contact with a green physical object.

Please do not mistake this for a serious psychosemantic doctrine, though it resembles some claims that have been offered as serious psychosemantics. I believe that its two important elements—"normally" in the unabashedly teleological sense and "caused"—will play an important role in the ultimate psychosemantics, and I will rely on each of them in what follows, but surely there is a good deal more to the visual representation of a color property, and here that further complexity will remain a set of open questions.

2 THE INDEPENDENCE OF QUALIA FROM CONSCIOUSNESS IN ANY MORE CENTRAL SENSE

It is time for an important word on the relation between qualia in my present strict sense and awareness or introspective consciousness (see again my remarks on problem (H) in chapter 1) and on the relation between both and "what it's like."

I said in introducing my strict Lewisian sense of "quale" that one registers such a quale whenever one perceives a colored object as such. Yet my term "registers" is to be understood very weakly. For some of our perceivings are un- or subconscious in the sense that we are unaware of achieving them (chapter 2). Armstrong (1980) gives the well-known example of the long-distance truck driver who is absentmindedly driving on automatic pilot (so to speak) while thinking of something entirely different; the driver "comes to" and suddenly realizes that he has driven for miles without any awareness of what he was doing. Yet he must have perceived the bends in the road, the road signs, the stop lights, and so on. Suppose that he did in fact stop at a red light. Presumably, the light looked red rather than green to him; that is the only reason he would have stopped. So, in the strict sense of the term, he was presented with a red quale; a subregion of his visual field had redness as its phenomenal or qualitative character. But the driver was not aware of any such thing; it was an un- or subconscious perceiving, entirely unintrospected.[9]

Yet some philosophers, at least, might be loath to credit the truck driver with having had a sensory *experience* of red; after all, he was entirely unaware of his perceptual encounter with the stop light. As remarked in chapter 2, certainly there is a sense in which one has not experienced phenomenal red, or *felt* pain, unless one is aware of the redness or the pain. To experience a sensation in this fuller sense, one must both have the relevant quale and notice it introspectively.

(There is a powerful, instinctive objection to the inner-sense theory of awareness that arises from missing the present point. Its main, if tacit, premise is that the mere addition of a higher-order monitoring to an entirely nonqualitative mental state could not possibly bring a *quale* into being. And that premise is plainly true. But the inner-sense theorist hardly need hold that monitoring does bring qualia into being. The monitoring only makes the subject aware of a quale that was there, independently, in the first place. Again, the inner-sense theory is simply not a theory of what makes a state qualitative in the first place.)

What, then, of "what it's like"? That phrase is now ambiguous, as between phenomenal character, i.e., a quale in the strict sense, and the conscious experience of such a quale, or rather what one knows in virtue of having such an experience. (And like the plural "qualia" itself, "what it's like" has a deplorably more general use, as an umbrella term for whatever one find puzzling about consciousness, subjectivity, etc.) It is long past time to recognize (as I said in note 3 to this chapter) that the phrase "what it's like" is now worse than useless: it is positively pernicious and harmful, because nothing whatever is clarified or explained by reference to it, and its tokening as a buzzword typically sends the struggling mind of even the most talented philosopher into yet another affect-driven tailspin of confusing a welter of distinct issues. So, please, just say no. (None of this will stop me from devoting a good deal of chapter 5 to the "what it's like" locution, but I will do so very carefully and in a critical rather than knee-jerk manner.)

But now to some serious difficulties for my view of qualia in the strict sense, raised by inverted-spectrum hypotheses.

3 INVERTED SPECTRUM

Here is the problem (since the "inverted spectrum" hypothesis is so familiar, I will expound it only very briefly): (1) It seems conceivable that someone might have her internal spectrum inverted with respect to everyone else's, having green sensations when the rest of us have red, yellow when we have blue, and so on. And this could be behaviorally undetectable: if the victim has had the condition from birth, she will have learned the public-language color words inversely and so compensated, growing up to call red things "red" and blue things "blue."[10] Indeed, as I and others have argued elsewhere, contrary to verificationists and Wittgensteinians, such inversion *is* perfectly conceivable.[11] But (2) if (1) is right, then it is just as conceivable that the human population should have been evenly split (50-50) between "normal" percipients and inversion victims—indeed, it may even be so split in real life.[12] But then (3) in such a population, the normal/victim distinction breaks down; half the people sense in one way when prompted by red physical objects, half in the other way, and there is no saying which way of sensing is correct or right. (Call this the "aggravatedly split inverted spectrum" hypothesis.)

And here is the rub: if (3) is right, then there is no such thing as sensing in "the" way normally or typically produced in us by red objects. So, it seems, phenomenal redness cannot be explicated in terms of sensing in "that" way.[13]

One can take a very tough line (slightly less tough than the toughest line of all, which is to deny (1)): reject (3). Some people are just wrong; half the population see red correctly, while the other half are still victims, deviants.[14] But this seems pretty desperate. Imaginably, there might be some special explanation of, and ontological ground for, the asymmetry, as if we were to find some separately identifiable genetic defect in the "victims" that correlated with and explained their spectrum difference, but just as imaginably, there might be no defect at all. Even then we might settle for skepticism (if we shun verificationism as zealously as we should). But now we may further imagine multiple, chaotic inversions, so that different people have many different internal spectra. This seems to show, more generally, that we cannot expect *any* regular connection between phenomenal colors and physical colors; worse and worse.

A more promising strategy in response to the objection is simply to deny the *metaphysical* possibility of aggravatedly split inverted spectra. (I will call this just "the tough line," since it is tough but not very tough.) Since earlier I insisted on conceding that inverted spectrum is conceptually possible, this move might have gone overlooked. But as Kripke (1972) has taught us, conceptual possibility, mere noncontradictoriness, is far from entailing bona fide metaphysical possibility, for the latter is constrained by some physical natures and essences, which cannot be known a priori. And physical natures and essences are just what are at stake in the present discussion. Thus we may hold that although inverted spectra are not only imaginable and "conceivable" in every psychological sense but logically possible as well, they are no more metaphysically possible than is the distinctness of water from H_2O or lightning from electrical discharge.

This strategy is encouraged by the well-known structural problems faced by anyone who tries to describe an actual spectrum inversion in any detail: not just any one-one mapping of hues onto hues will go behaviorally undetected. Indeed, it has been argued that if a proposed inversion preserves all discriminative relations as well as the total number of discriminable presentations, then it must detectably alter some gradation of hue, brightness, or tone.[15] Thus it is far from obvious that an aggravatedly split inverted spectrum is metaphysically possible, i.e., compatible with the natures of real colors and color sensations all taken together.

The tough line is defensible, I think, and may well be correct. But it is not *fun*. Let us daringly concede more, and live a little.

Fortunately, before we are forced to grant the troublesome (3), there is an only moderately tough line. This is a weakening of the tough line that grants even the metaphysical possibility of a half-and-half population difference but is augmented by an argument to show, *à la* the very tough line, that an aggravatedly split inverted spectrum is not possible. The idea is that we can grant a population-split hypothesis, whether lopsided or even, so long as there are independent grounds for drawing the normal/victim distinction. If it is put to us that a population has (not, of course, exhibits) a spectrum distinction, we may ask which subgroup responds to red things with color sensations other than those normally produced by red things, and if there is an answer based on genetic or other biological defect, we will understand and accept this answer, for it addresses our concern for normalcy. But if there is no such answer and the idea is simply (3), that there is an even split or a chaotic fragmentation in no way tied to any normal psychological response to red things, then although we may conceptually understand the hypothesis, we have no reason to count it as metaphysically possible.[16]

This last is the operative claim. The point is not a conceptual one about intelligibility, for charges of unintelligibility are almost never true. And as I have hinted, I think conceptual analysis is of little use in the study of color. In any case the present topic is metaphysics. The point is rather that if the nature of one's internal spectrum is (metaphysically) a matter of the normal causes of one's experiences, then although an inverted spectrum is possible—in that in looking at a red object I may sense greenly, i.e., have the experience normally caused by looking at green objects—an aggravatedly split inverted spectrum may still not be metaphysically possible because of a breakdown in normalcy. On this view, a population that harbors no distinctive set of biologically normal visual responses to colored objects does not experience the world in color, because it is in the a posteriori nature of color sensation to be the normal effect of a certain environmental stimulus. This in itself is not an implausible thesis.[17]

We must struggle to separate metaphysical issues from conceptual issues and from epistemic issues. One may still be tempted to protest that even if science should establish that all actual color sensations can be classified as normal effects (which is not to say that they always have their corresponding normal causes or even that they do more often than not), we can easily imagine species that have kaleidoscopically split internal spectra but do not afford any biological distinction between normal and abnormal visual responses to colored objects.

But imaginability (or seeming imaginability) is beside the point. Given a kind of thing or property and its scientific/metaphysical nature, we can *always* imagine a thing or property of that kind lacking that nature: water but not H_2O, lightning but not electrical discharge. More generally, we can almost always look at a characteristic consequence of some metaphysical theory and imagine it to be false (unless we ourselves are so persuaded of that theory that our imaginative powers are lassooed[18]). Granted, imaginability creates a presumption in favor of possibility,[19] but this presumption is overridden by a good theory of a scientific nature when we can get one. The question is whether our theory is a good one, not whether someone can imagine its being false.[20]

We may be troubled further by skeptical worries: Confronted by an alien species that exhibits some fairly even physiological split, how could we know which of its members' states are "normal" responses to whatever? And for that matter, given a species that exhibits an undoubted normal/abnormal distinction, how could we know that a spectrum inversion is constituted by that distinction?

Perhaps we could not. It might prove forever impossible to tell. But only a verificationist would be particularly troubled by this, and if one *is* a verificationist, one ought to stop being one. Besides, it is more likely that exobiologists studying our refractory species would in time devise some ingenious test for normalcy or for spectrum inversion. (As Hilary Putnam pointed out years ago [1965], history reveals one liability of branding some hypothesis as unverifiable: quite often some inventive experimentalist comes along and verifies it.)

Thus the hegemony of representation is not yet refuted by inverted-spectrum hypotheses; so far as has been shown, qualia supervene on representation. But we will be dragged back to problems of spectrum inversion in chapter 6.

4 AUSTRALIAN TRANSLATIONS AND KOBES'S OBJECTION

In *Consciousness* I did not stop with the contention that apparent phenomenal individuals are intentional objects. I added the following further order of battle. A complication here is that it is partly independent of, indeed cuts across, the psychosemantic schema as posited in section 1 of this chapter, and Kobes attacked it independently. So I will formulate it in its own terms and only parenthetically remind the reader of its relation to my psychosemantic schema.

(1)   One model (due to Place and Smart) for intentional inexistents that answer to existential quantifications inside psychological operators is that of "being in one's mind *as if*" ("It is in my mind [visually] as if a pointy green object is before me"; I take this to be one version of the more basic claim that one's visual state represents the object, though that claim does not depend on this particular implementation).

(2)   This model is a good one, for it squares both with the qualitative character of experience and with the empirical explanation of why we experience the phenomenal individuals we do. It also makes good syntactic sense of the apparatus of reference to, and quantification over, phenomenal individuals, which adverbialism can hardly begin to do. (It

still requires a psychosemantics of the sort I have begged off providing.)

(3) The model is counterfactual. And so it should be tested against a going semantics for counterfactuals.

But first,

(4) Since the "as if" locution is elliptical, the exact counterfactual antecedent and consequent need filling in; let us expand the "as if" thus: "as *one would be sensing* if a *physical* green object is before one."

(5) The best going semantics for counterfactuals is a possible-worlds semantics, and a possible-worlds explication of the "as if" model for phenomenal individuals also provides strikingly for the referential apparatus mentioned in (1), the references being to objects existing in or "at" the alternative worlds.

(6) The otherworldly objects are physical at those worlds, so we need not worry anywhere about *nonphysical* phenomenal individuals.

Granted,

(7) We need to explain the physical natures of their qualitative properties in their own containing worlds.

Also,

(8) A Stalnakerian similarity relation that figures in the truth-evaluation of counterfactuals will have to be adjusted accordingly.[21]

Parenthetically,

(9) When one eventually turns to the homogeneity question mentioned in chapter 1 as problem (G), (9) and (10) are complicated by the fact, if it is one, that "homogeneity" really means homeomerousness, but let us here say no more of such horrors.

In his (robustly) critical study of *Consciousness,* Bernard Kobes (1991) offers several counterexamples to my account as developed through item (6), in particular to my unpacking of "as if." (The matter is complicated by the fact that my account was meant in part to handle homogeneity problems in particular, but Kobes's counterexamples are important quite apart from that.[22]) First,

> If [W.G.L.'s protagonist] Leopold is a deuteranope (i.e. red-green color-blind), he may be sensing as he would be sensing if a . . . green external patch were present to him, but he would not have a . . . green visual sensation. (Kobes 1991, 154)

This shows the need to drop my formula "as *he* [Leopold] would be sensing if a green physical object were present to *him*" in favor of "as *one* would be sensing if a green physical object were present to one"—it being assumed, as Kobes suggests, that one is "normal"—or perhaps more directly, in favor of "as he would be sensing if a green physical object were present to him and he were normal." (I had crassly failed to make either distinction.) It seems noncircular and independently justifiable to suppose that color-blindness is abnormal, because the victim lacks a discriminative capacity that most people have (hence that is readily available from Mother Nature) and discriminative capacities presumably are psychologically and biologically good.

But now,

> Suppose we discover that a certain kind of direct electrochemical stimulation of the primary visual cortex gives rise in normal people to an entirely novel color sensation—call it "newhue." We further discover that, for neurological reasons, no stimulation of the retina can give rise to newhue sensations. This amounts to discovering that no physical object could, compatibly with our natural laws, be newhue. Yet we can get people to agree about whether newhue is closer to orange than to violet, and whether someone has a visual sensation as of a newhue elephant. . . .

Lycan's account, as emended, assigns to the sentence "Leopold has a newhue visual sensation" the analysis "Leopold is sensing as he *would be sensing* if a newhue physical patch were presented to him under normal conditions." But it's nomologically impossible for there to be a newhue physical patch presented to Leopold. (Kobes 1991, 154–155; italics in the original)

I have several replies to make to this, but they are not overwhelmingly powerful.[23] In any case, Kobes only turns to his third example, which has considerably greater intuitive force. I will not quote him this time, because the example (that of a species called Visipiks) was originally directed at the homogeneity issue, but it generalizes fast. Take any species that characteristically and normally responds to green objects by having something other than a green sensation. Think of a population, the Antigreens, to whom green physical objects are simply invisible. Or perhaps we are in the Land of Color-Sound Conversion, whose inhabitants characteristically and normally respond to green objects by hearing a shrill whine. Kobes's point is that in any such case, the alien protagonist will sense as *it* characteristically senses when confronted with a green object under normal conditions, namely, *other than* greenly, and so I am truly counterexampled.

Notice, though, that my Kobesian description of these scenarios has tacitly countenanced something that I officially do not grant. If members of the alien species in question normally (in the teleological sense) respond to green objects in a characteristic way *w*, then according to my psychosemantic schema as posited earlier in this chapter, a member of that species who responds in way *w* is sensing greenly and having a visual experience as of a green object, period. So I do not concede to Kobes that an Antigreen could find green objects "simply invisible," or that members of the Conversion society would sense green objects by hearing a shrill whine *as opposed to* having a green visual sensation (though the sensation might double as an auditory whine, depending). So I find Kobes' third sort of example unconvincing in light of my psychosemantic schema. But let us suspend this objection and assume the possibility of Kobes's scenario for the sake of evaluating the "as if" analysis and stage (6) on their own terms. Once we have done so, his counterexample still seems decisive.

One might try pegging my counterfactual account to our own species, thus: Given any organism of any species anywhere, what it is for that organism to have a green sensation is for the organism to be sensing as *we* (normal human beings) would be sensing *in the actual world* were a green object present to us. Kobes's Visipiks (if any) and the Antigreens and Converters do not have green sensations when confronted by green objects, precisely because they do not sense *as we do* in such circumstances. This move makes "green sensation" into a rigid designator whose reference is fixed by allusion to ourselves in the actual world (which is fine in itself; the word "green" is our word, after all). The move thereby entails that *necessarily,* whatever creature has a green sensation under any circumstances must be having one of the sort with which we normally respond in this world to (hypothetically) green objects, but again, this seems right.

The trouble with this rigidifying move is that the same sort of counterexample inverts to match it.[24] Suppose that there is an alien species whose members' vision is much like ours except that there is an extra hue that they can see under certain special lighting and reflectance conditions. We human beings know that about the aliens, and we coin the word "Martianhue" for the extra color, but it is nomologically impossible for creatures with brains like ours to experience this color under any conditions. Then one of the aliens might be experiencing Martianhue, but it would certainly not be sensing in the way we normal human beings would be sensing in the presence of a Martianhue physical object, since we do not respond visually to Martianhue objects at all.

Ouch. But Kobes's victory here leaves a puzzle—for anyone, not just for my "as if" theory—because my previous stages (3) to (5) are still very plausible: if I am having a pointy green afterimage, it still sounds perfectly right to say that I am sensing "as though" a similarly green object were present to me, and that my experience is "as of" such an object. Even one who held an unreconstructed Russellian sense-datum theory should find it so. If (6) is incorrect as a spelling out of the Australian "as if," then what spelling out is right?

Unexpectedly, since my original exchange with Kobes, new light has been shed on "as if" locutions by Mark Crimmins (1992). It should be of considerable interest to linguists. For Crimmins has challenged the ellipsis hypothesis I instinctively presumed in stage (4) above: that "S is V-ing as if P" merely abbreviates "S is V-ing as S *would be V-ing* if P." And Crimmins is right: "Leopold is running as if a lion were chasing him" does not mean simply, that Leopold is running as he would be running if a lion were chasing him, because Leopold might be so cowardly that if a lion really were chasing him, he would just become paralyzed with fear and sink whimpering to the ground, waiting to be eaten. Similarly, "Jay spends money as if there were no tomorrow" does not mean that Jay spends money as he would be spending it if there really were no tomorrow, for who knows what Jay would be doing if there really, literally, were no tomorrow?

Thus Kobes's Visipik type of counterexample, while still a counterexample, is but one instance of a more general syntactic phenomenon. It is a counterexample to my suggestion that both "Leopold has a pointy green patch in his visual field" and "Leopold is visually sensing as if a pointy green object were before him" mean that Leopold is visually sensing as he would be sensing if a pointy green object were before him. But Crimmins's point shows that Kobes's Visi-piks are not a counterexample to the claim that the two sentences just mentioned are (in some strong sense) equivalent, whatever they might mean *other* than that Leopold is visually sensing as he would be sensing if a pointy green object were before him.

What, then, is the correct general analysis of "*S* is *V*-ing as if *P*"? Crimmins has little to say on this score (for such is not part of his project). He suggests that "in general, a statement that it is as if such-and-such, expresses a claim to the effect that a relevant actual situation is relevantly like relevant hypothetical situations in which such-and-such is the case" (Crimmins 1992, 248–249); after that he offers just a few more specific proposals directed toward his own explicandum, the notion of "tacit belief."[25] For our own purposes, we are left only with the notion of relevant similarity per se.

On this spare model, "Leopold is visually sensing as if a pointy green object were before him" would mean, in the first instance, that Leopold is visually sensing in a way that is "relevantly like" what would be going on if a pointy green object were before him, where this does not in turn mean that he is sensing in the way he himself would be sensing on that same condition. This by itself gives us little more guidance than did Smart's original topic-neutral gloss: "There is something going on which is like what is going on when . . . there is a . . . [pointy green physical object] illuminated in good light in front of me." We do know, on the basis of Crimmins-style counterexamples, that the relevant similarity in question is not pegged to the subject of the target sentence. Rather, it seems to depend on a stereotype of some sort: "Leopold is running as *a typical person* would be running if a lion were chasing that person," to give a crude first approximation. But it does not help much just to apply this gloss to a sensation sentence: "Leopold is visually sensing as a typical person would be sensing if a pointy green object were before that person," for this says virtually nothing until the operative respects of similarity are spelled out in some detail.

Thus, although by abandoning the ellipsis interpretation of "as if" I have evaded Kobes's objection, I have yet to replace that interpretation with any compelling substitute that also avoids the objection, and so the Australian "as if" issue is unresolved despite the so far unimpugned plausibility of the original "as if" paraphrase.

I will leave the matter here, except to remind the reader that my fundamental claim about qualia strictly so called, that they are intentional items, does not depend on the "as if" issue, because the latter is only one possible implementation of the former. I continue to believe that there exists a correct implementation and that whatever it is, the right explicans will make reference to nonactual colored objects. Thus stage (7) of my program will remain as before, as will my view of the ontological status of qualia, though it is now unclear what sorts of objects the bearers of the qualia will be. Also, once I am permitted to import the psychosemantic schema of section 1, I will be able to deal more forcefully with puzzle cases of Kobes's general kind, because some of them will be ruled out as only epistemic, rather than real metaphysical, possibilities.

We will return to the topic of qualia in chapter 6. But next I will fit the theme of this chapter into that of the last.

A Limited Defense of Phenomenal Information

My purpose in this chapter is to assess one distinctive and important defense of materialism against Nagel's and Jackson's knowledge argument (disparaged in chapter 3), that of Laurence Nemirow (1980, 1990) and David Lewis (1983a, 1990) (see also Teller 1992). Though I have some sympathy with their view, I will argue that, as advertised, the argument is unsuccessful and that Nemirow and Lewis should shift to my own point of attack instead.

1   THE DIALECTIC

Jackson (1982, 128) offers the now familiar example of Mary, the brilliant color scientist trapped in an entirely black-and-white laboratory (even she herself is painted black and white). Working through her modem and her computer monitor, she becomes scientifically omniscient as regards the physics and chemistry of color, the neurophysiology of color vision, and every other conceivably relevant scientific fact; we may even suppose that she becomes scientifically omniscient, period. Yet when she is finally released from her captivity and ventures into the outside world, she sees colors for the first time and learns something: namely, she learns what it is like to see red, blue, ochre and the rest of the gang. Thus she has acquired information that is (by hypothesis) outside the whole domain of science—intrinsically subjective, phenomenal information.

Nemirow and Lewis respond by agreeing that Mary learns something new, adequately expressed by the now cant phrase "what it's like," but then they move to deny that knowing what it's like to be in a particular sensory state is a propositional matter, a knowing-that. Rather, according to Nemirow and Lewis, "knowing what it's like" is only a knowing-how, an ability. Nemirow thinks it is an ability to imagine—in the case of a color, the ability to visualize that color. Lewis (1990, 515–516) adds that it can also comprehend abilities to remember experiences, to recognize similar ones when they occur, and to imagine related experiences that one has never had. Thus what Mary gains is not a special, perspectival sort of phenomenal information; it is not information at all.

As I mentioned in note 25 to chapter 3, I could live with Nemirow's and Lewis's bold contention; indeed, I think they are half right. But for what it is worth, I believe they are also and importantly half wrong. I will argue that they have posed a false dichotomy: between phenomenal information in a materialistically objectionable sense and mere nonpropositional abilities.

To begin, let me set out some positive arguments for the claim that what Mary gains is indeed propositional knowledge and not just a set of abilities. Later I will evaluate those arguments in light of two distinctions that Nemirow and Lewis have ignored.

2 TEN ARGUMENTS AGAINST NEMIROW AND LEWIS

Argument 1: From Meaning and Syntax

Indirect-question clauses are closely related to "that" clauses, both in meaning and grammatically. In particular,

instances of "*S* knows wh- . . ." are related to "*S* knows that
. . .": "*S* knows where *X* *V*s" is true in virtue of *S*'s knowing
that *X* *V*s at *p*, where '*p*' suitably names some place; "*S*
knows when *X* *V*s" is true in virtue of *S*'s knowing that *X* *V*s
at *t*, where "*t*" suitably names some time; "*S* knows who *V*s"
is true in virtue of *S*s knowing that *N* *V*s, where '*N*' suitably
names some person. ("Suitably" in these formulations hides
a multitude of technicalities, but they do not affect the
present issue.[1]) There are close syntactic relations as
well: consider "when"/"then," "where"/"there," "whither"/
"thither," and the like.[2]

On this model, "*S* knows what it's like to see blue"
means roughly "*S* knows that it is like *Q* to see blue," where
"*Q*" suitably names some inner phenomenal property or
condition. Therefore, Nemirow and Lewis cannot strictly
and literally use the "knowing what it's like" locution; they
must say that the Farrell's, Nagel's, and Jackson's formulation is erroneous and that those authors have mistaken a
knowing-how for a knowing-what. If the rest of us continue
to think that what Mary learns is *literally* what it is like to see
the various colors, we should resist Nemirow and Lewis.

Nemirow anticipates a similar point and responds that
the phrase "what it's like" is "a 'pseudo-singular term' . . .
that has the grammatical form of a singular term but, on
analysis, does not even purport to refer. Like . . . the term
'sake' in the sentence, 'She did it for her country's sake'. . . .
The [ability] analysis should forestall the temptation to treat
the expression 'what it's like' as a referring expression in virtue of its grammatical form" (1990, 494–495).

Well, true, the ability analysis should forestall that
temptation *if* the analysis is supported by convincing syntactic and semantic evidence. Grammatical appearance can
mask a strikingly different underlying logical reality. But
here as elsewhere, the burden of proof lies with the theorist
who insists that reality differs from appearance. And in the
present case, the topic is grammar and logic, so the relevant

evidence would be syntactic and semantic, of the sort deployed by linguists and linguistic semanticists; purely philosophical wish-fulfillment does not count. Yet Nemirow has provided no counterevidence at all to the standard linguistic grounds for thinking that "wh- . . ." complements are derived from "that"-clauses. So my temptation to treat "what it's like" as a referring expression is as yet unhindered.

Argument 2: From Embedding

Loar reprises a famous argument of Geach's against emotivism about moral judgments:

> One can have knowledge not only of the form "pains feel like such and such" but also of the form "*if* pains feel like such and such then Q." Perhaps you could get away with saying that the former expresses (not a genuine judgment but) the mere possession of recognitional know-how. There seems however to be no comparable way of accounting for the embedded occurrence of "feels like such and such" in the latter; it seems to introduce a predicate with a distinctive content. (1990, 86)

We may add that conditionals and other compound sentences containing phenomenal clauses can be used in reasoning; e.g., a bodily-sensation analogue of Mary might token Loar's conditional prior to her release, and then, upon her finding out that pains do feel like such and such, she may correctly deduce that Q.

Argument 3: From Possibility Elimination

As Lewis himself says (1990, 505), the acquisition of "information" is often conceived of as the elimination of possibilities: to receive a piece of information is to rule out a particular class of possible worlds as candidates for being *one's own* world. (Finally to narrow the candidates down to just one would be to become omniscient.) And sets of possible worlds constitute, or at least correspond to, propositions: intuitively, a given set corresponds to proposition p iff it is the class of worlds at which p holds.

But when Mary is released from her colorless room and undergoes her epiphany, surely she does eliminate some possibilities, e.g., that visual yellow might look phenomenally one way or another (say what we call "pink") instead of the way it actually does look. The possible worlds she rules out form a set. A set of worlds is a proposition. So for some proposition p_q, she has learned that p_q.

Though Lewis himself suggested this argument, he does not rebut it directly. He does say that "the alternative possibilities must be unthinkable beforehand":

I cannot present to myself in thought a range of alternative possibilities about what it might be like to taste Vegemite. That is because I cannot imagine either what it *is* like to taste Vegemite, or any alternative way that it *might* be like but in fact isn't. . . . I can't even pose the question that phenomenal information is supposed to answer: is it this way or that? (Lewis 1990, 512)

But this does not address the point made above, which was just that *there are* multiple possibilities. My argument does not require that Mary or anyone else have imagined those possibilities in advance, or even that anyone would ever be able to do so.

Argument 4: From Theoretical Knowledge

It would be perverse to claim that bare experience can provide us *only* with various practical abilities, and never with theoretical knowledge. By being shown an unfamiliar color, I acquire information about its similarities and compatibilities with other colors, and its effects on other of our mental states: surely I seem to be acquiring certain facts about that color and the visual experience of it. (Levin 1986, 479)

(Of course, *Mary* would acquire no such facts, since, being scientifically omniscient, she would already have known them. Levin is speaking of the rest of us.)

Nemirow obliquely responds to this:

> In reasoning from what an experience is like, a person begins by imagining particular experiences, and draws specific inferences about actual or future sensory experiences, none of which is itself critical to the function of the imagination. Such lines of inference in turn begin to account for the general utilities of imagining that cause imagining to appear to grant direct access to the essential qualities of experience. (1990, 496)

Nemirow seems to grant that we "draw inferences" from our imaginings. Why does this not amount to endorsing Levin's argument, rather than refuting it? Perhaps the point is (in Sellarsian jargon) that it is the imagin*ings* or events of imagining that serve as premises in the inferences, rather than the imagin*eds*, or propositional contents imagined. But when Levin suggests that by being shown an unfamiliar color, we acquire information about its relations to other colors, etc., she could not mean that the event of our *doing the imagining* shows us these things and licenses the relevant inferences; rather, it is (for all Nemirow and Lewis have argued) *what* we succeed in imagining that does this. And, one would think, contents that afford inferences to propositional conclusions are themselves propositional.

Argument 5: From the Empiricist Residue

The British Empiricists believed that all empirical knowledge was based on purely phenomenal knowledge involving phenomenal concepts. Now, although there are few British Empiricists left these days, why should we reject even the last vestige of their view? Is not *some* empirical knowledge, even the smallest occasional bit, based on beliefs about the phenomenal character of one's experience? If so, then there are such beliefs, and, plausibly, Mary could not have had phenomenal-color beliefs before her release, because, as the Empiricists argued, one must have phenomenal experience in order to have phenomenal concepts, and one must have phenomenal concepts in order to have phenomenal beliefs (Levin 1986).

Argument 6: From "Important Cognitive Differences"

Levin defines what she calls a "direct recognitional capacity" as "an ability to know that one is in a particular [mental] state without making inferences, . . . simply by applying one's concept of that mental state to the experiences at hand," and she points out that people do sometimes have such knowledge (1986, 479–480).[3] If we have direct recognitional capacities that other species, or even other human beings, do not have, then is it not reasonable to explain those differences *in factual knowings* by appeal to differences in our knowledge of phenomenal facts about experience?

Argument 7: From the Best Explanation of the Abilities

For that matter, our imaginative and other abilities themselves call for explanation. Is not our ability to visualize red or blue best explained by our factual knowledge of what it is like to see those colors? Consider our more familiar quotidian imaginative abilities. For example, I can visualize my mother-in-law's face when she is not present or the front of my house when I am out of town. Those abilities are well explained by the uncontroversial fact of my knowing what my mother-in-law and the front of my house look like, and there is nothing mysterious about these items of knowledge, since I can express them descriptively in some detail. Why should my knowing what it is like to see red or blue be explained differently?[4]

There is one difference that might be thought relevant. Though mothers-in-law and houses can be described in public natural languages, what it is like to experience a sensation of red or of blue cannot, except at best in comparative or analogical terms. As Nemirow points out (1990, 493), that ineffability is well explained by Nemirow's and Lewis's "ability" thesis. But it can also be variously explained by friends of phenomenal information—notoriously by Russell, for example. Nemirow and Lewis have no monopoly on ineffability.[5] So the ineffability difference has not yet been shown to impugn our explanation of the imaginative abilities.

Argument 8: From Attempting-to-Describe

One can *try* to convey the taste of pineapple to someone who has never eaten pineapple, though probably without much success. It certainly feels as though there is something to describe, if only we could find the words, and some of the descriptions we offer get at the taste better than others do. If Nemirow and Lewis are right, this sort of attempt is utterly misguided, and its seeming partial success is completely illusory, for there is nothing to describe; description is propositional. Nemirow and Lewis owe us at least an explanation of the illusion.

Argument 9: From Comparisons

Consider explicitly comparative descriptions of phenomenal qualities. Hydrogen sulfide smells (as I recall) like rotten eggs.[6] On the assumption that this statement is true, what is its truth-maker? Presumably just that rotten eggs smell a certain way and that hydrogen sulfide smells the same way. This could be relativized to a person and a brief period of time: what it is like for S to smell hydrogen sulfide during a time interval Δ*t* is exactly what it is like for *S* to smell rotten eggs during Δ*t*. But this formulation seems to treat "what it's like" as a matter of fact, even if as an ineffable fact, and the facts in question per se are not about imagining but about actually smelling. And what is factual is propositional.

Argument 10: From Success and Failure

As Nemirow concedes (1990, 497), imagining can be successful or unsuccessful; indeed, correct or incorrect. I can visualize my boyhood home in New Jersey and be fairly certain that the house did look as I am imagining, but then find, upon checking a period photograph, that I have got it wrong. Imagining is a form of representation. Therefore, if to know "what it's like" to experience phenomenal red is in large part to be able to imagine experiencing red, presumably this means imagining correctly rather than incorrectly. I would not be counted as knowing what it is like to see red—especially by a proponent of Nemirow's and Lewis's ability hypothesis—if, when I tried to imagine such an experience, I always visualized what is in fact blue or yellow. And therefore, there is such a thing as getting "what it's like" right, representing truly rather than falsely, from which it seems to follow that knowing "what it's like" is knowing a truth.[7]

3 TWO DISTINCTIONS

Thus a vigorous case can be made against Nemirow and Lewis.[8] But now let us seek the middle path. Let us revisit the notion of a quale, in our carefully strict (C. I.) Lewisian sense of the term. On my view as defended in the previous chapter, a quale is a represented property, an intentional object; *S*'s visual sensation represents the tomato (whether correctly or falsely) as having the color red. The visual sensation represents a state of affairs in which an external object, or its physical surface, has a certain intrinsic property. Perhaps this property is real, objective physical redness and could be described and investigated by physics. Or perhaps (if my Armstrongian color realism is mistaken) there is not really any such property as "objective physical redness," but in that case S's sensing is unveridical and portrays something that does not exist.

Recall section 2 of the previous chapter, in which I distinguished between *merely* registering a quale, in the manner of Armstrong's long-distance truck driver, and consciously doing so, i.e., being aware of it. Recall also the ambiguity of "what it's like," as between phenomenal character (i.e., a quale in our strict sense) and the conscious experience of such a quale or the introspective *knowledge of* phenomenal character. That is the first distinction I emphasize in this section. Remember, *it is important, both for psychologists and for philosophers, to separate questions about qualia from questions about awareness and introspective consciousness.* Failure to notice the difference has led to some considerable confusion in research on consciousness.

Now consider the business of internal awareness or introspection. On the inner-sense theory defended in chapter 2, introspection is the operation of one or more internal monitors or scanners, and when they operate, a creature's monitors emit representations as their output, second-order representations of the subject's own first-order psychological states. This hypothesis yields my second present distinction, already familiar from chapter 3: if indeed there is second-order representing of first-order states, including states that include qualia in my strict sense, then as in any case of representation, each introspective second-order representation has both a *referent* and a *mode of presentation* under which the referent is exhibited; it presents a feature of the first-order state in question but also presents that feature in a certain way, under a particular guise.

CHAPTER FIVE

As before, think of an introspective representation as a token in one of the subject's languages of thought, his or her Introspectorese. As an immediate consequence of the operation of one of S's internal monitors, we might say, S tokens a semantically primitive mental word for the type of first-order state being inwardly sensed. And since its inferential and/or conceptual role would be unique to its subject, in that no other subject could deploy a functionally similar representation whose designatum was that (the subject's) very same first-order state-token, the introspective word would certainly not be synonymous with any primitive or composite expression of public English, even though it would *corefer* with some English expressions. As we saw in chapter 3, it would be a name that only its actual user could use to name its actual referent.

4 PHENOMENAL INFORMATION

And now we can see why Nemirow and Lewis are both right and wrong about phenomenal information. They are right in that no special phenomenal facts, in the coarse-grained sense, are introduced by the "what it's like" locution. For all that has been shown by Nagel and Jackson, neither qualia nor our awareness of qualia require any surd in nature or any unscientistic ontology.

But Nemirow and Lewis are also wrong, in that there is a perfectly good sense of "information," more finely grained than that of "fact," in which there is after all phenomenal information, indeed, phenomenal information inaccessible to objective, third-person science.[9] Upon her release, Mary learns that actually to experience red is like . . . ploiku!— where my sign-design "ploiku" stands in lieu of whatever mental morpheme is actually tokened by Mary's introspector in making its report. (Again, this morpheme cannot be expressed in standard English, even though it corefers with expressions like "Mary's being appeared to redly" and "Mary's being in a perceptual state of the red-presenting sort" and "Mary's hosting cognitive goings-on [so-and-so].") Think again of my coming to believe, upon recovering from my amnesia, that *I* am undereducated, even though (on the basis of reading the standard biographies) I have always believed that W.G.L. is undereducated. In the functional and/or computational sense, I certainly do acquire some new information, and my cognitive powers are greatly enhanced, even though in the coarse-grained extensional sense I have not learned any new fact. I relearn the same fact in a new, behavior-affecting guise. And propositional-attitude constructions in natural language mark this phenomenon by offering a choice between two starkly different complement clauses—"that W.G.L. is undereducated" versus "that he himself is undereducated"—in that perfectly good sense, different information ascribed. Hereafter I shall speak of *computational information,* meaning the fine-grained type distinguished by functional modes of presentation, as opposed to *coarse factual information,* meaning the information corresponding to facts in the coarse-grained sense that ignores modes of presentation.

5   THE ARGUMENTS AGAIN

Multiplied by each other, my two distinctions require a four-fold approach to arguments for and against phenomenal information. For in any case of sensing, there is (1) at least one quale (strictly so called), a qualitative intentional object, such as the alleged objective redness of S's tomato. There is also (2) the mode of presentation under which the represented property is represented (in S's case the visual-redness mode, as opposed, say, to some scientific description of the color property, if the property is indeed a real property of objects and has a scientific description). If the subject is consciously aware of doing the sensing, there will also be (3) his or her introspector's internal representation of the sensing itself, and (4) the special introspective mode of presentation under which the sensing is represented, as opposed to a third-person computational or neurobiological description.

Thus there are potentially four types of information involved in any sensing: coarse factual information as represented in the form of a quale, the computational information that incorporates the distinctive sensory mode of presentation, the coarse factual information recorded by one's introspector, and the computational information that incorporates the introspector's special mode of presenting the latter. In the case of *S* and her tomato, these are, respectively, that the tomato is red, where "red" occupies an extensional position and can be replaced by any correct description of objective redness, if any; that the tomato is red qua red as opposed to qua something from physics; that *S* herself is sensing in a visual-red way, where "sensing in a visual-red way" can be replaced by any correct description of the same state of affairs, such as a psychophysical description; and that *S* is having one of those . . . well, *those* sensations again, where the frustrated demonstrative can be replaced by nothing in English but only (*per impossibile*) by a lexeme of S-Introspectorese, such as "ploiku."

We saw in section 3 of this chapter that the phrase "what it's like" is ambiguous as between phenomenal character, i.e., a quale, and the conscious experience of such a quale. But the issue of "phenomenal information" as discussed by Farrell, Nagel, and Jackson and addressed by Nemirow and Lewis was raised as having to do with a *knowing,* a knowing whose object is already something mental, e.g., knowing what it is like to experience red, so the issue concerns only our third and fourth kinds of information.

It remains to run through the ten arguments of section 2 to see to what extent and exactly how their conclusions are vindicated by the present model. I will do this very quickly and not finish the job in any detail, for it is a fairly routine exercise to see that my notion of "computational information" does vindicate most of the conclusions of the ten arguments. As I have noted, "that" clauses are sometimes specialized for computational information, as opposed to merely coarse factual information (recall knowing "that H_2O is splashing" as opposed to "that water is splashing," or believing "that he is undereducated" as opposed to "that I am undereducated" when "he" and I are in fact the same person). Most of the ten arguments militate just for "that" clauses of the fine-grained computational sort, not for distinctive "phenomenal information" in the more alarming sense of coarse factual information, i.e., new facts. But the first three of the arguments have special features.

My introspective model more or less explains the data that afford argument 1, the argument from meaning and syntax. To know "what it's like" to experience visual red is to know introspectively that experiencing red is like *that,* like *ploiku;* it is to have computational information that has no English expression. The same applies to argument 2, from embedding. "Experiencing red is like that, ploiku" is a clause that can be embedded anywhere.

Argument 3, the argument from possibility elimination, requires qualification. For the possibility Mary eliminates, say that visual yellow might look phenomenally like what we call "pink," instead of the way it actually does look, is not a metaphysical possibility that outruns total science but rather is only a conceptual possibility whose negation supervenes on total science. So the worlds Mary rules out form at best a set of metaphysically impossible worlds, if such there be, and it is questionable whether a set of metaphysically impossible worlds constitutes propositional information in any decent sense.

But computational information does come to the rescue. Recall our pronominal examples. I can newly learn that the meeting will be held *here*, even though I already knew that the meeting will be held in room 215 and this room is in fact room 215, and I can newly come to believe that I am undereducated even though I already believe that W.G.L. is undereducated. In each case the "possibility" that I eliminate is a metaphysical impossibility. As we have seen, computational information is finer-grained than is coarse factual information, and its grain distinguishes between guises presenting the same fact. So the argument's premise is not strictly true: Mary does not eliminate any genuine metaphysical possibility. But doing so is not the only way of acquiring information; one can acquire computational information, expressible in a perfectly well-formed "that"-clause of the kind marked for fine computational individuation.

Argument 4, the argument from theoretical knowledge, is supported by my notion of computational information, for the information that Levin (1986) says I acquire when I am shown an unfamiliar color is seemingly gained by inference, and inference is computation rather than the mere obtaining of an abstract semantic relation. But as always, this entails nothing about learning a new "coarse" fact.

As can readily be checked, similar points hold of all the other arguments, 5 through 10. In each case, information is doing some work—inferential, explanatory, comparative, or whatever—but in each case, computational information suffices to complete that work and new, weird coarse factual information need not be posited.

6 LEWIS'S OWN ARGUMENTS AND THE THREAT OF EPIPHENOMENALISM

Lewis (1990, 512–514) has offered two direct arguments against phenomenal information, which need to be rebutted in light of the model I have offered. They are arguments from

queerness, specifically, charges that phenomenal information would have to be epiphenomenal in an objectionable
sense, since differences in phenomenal information would
(at best) find it hard to make a difference to the subject's
behavior.

The first argument is that learning to see colors affects
Mary's behavior in obvious ways, but if there were phenomenal information, such causal relations would be impossible.

Suppose the phenomenal aspect of the world had been otherwise, so that she gained different phenomenal information. Or
suppose the phenomenal aspect of the world had been absent altogether, as we materialists think it is. Would that have made the
slightest difference to what she did or said then or later? I think
not. Making a difference to what she does and says means, at
least in part, making a difference to the motions of the particles
of which she is composed. . . . But if something non-physical
sometimes makes a difference to the motions of physical particles, then physics as we know it is wrong. (Lewis 1990,
512–513)

Lewis concludes that, rather than flout physics, the friend of
phenomenal information should admit that the phenomenal
aspect is epiphenomenal, which is very bad.

If it were coarse factual information that were being
defended against Nemirow and Lewis, the charge of epiphenomenalism would have considerable force.[10] But computational information is itself individuated functionally, in
terms of some of its causes and causal powers themselves,
rather than solely in terms of its referents. (It is hardly surprising that I behave differently once I come to believe that I
am underpaid, and the computational information "that I
am underpaid" is distinguished from "that W.G.L. is underpaid" precisely in terms of functional differences.) So there
is no reason to doubt that computational information does
affect the motions of particles (at least by downward causation). Lewis's argument does not impugn the fine-grained
sort of phenomenal information I have defended here.

His second argument does not presuppose the empirical truth of "physics as we know it." He begins by concessively supposing that Mary's behavior does depend on some particular "phenomenal aspect of the world."

> Then we can describe the phenomenal aspect, if we know enough, in terms of its physical effects. It is that on which physical phenomena depend in such-and-such way. This descriptive handle will enable us to give lessons on it to the inexperienced. But in so far as we can give lessons on it, what we have is just parapsychology. That whereof we cannot learn except by having the experience still eludes us. (Lewis 1990, 513)

Lewis goes on to illustrate the dilemma in some detail. But it is essentially just this: If there is dependence of behavior on some aspect of the phenomenal, then "lessons" can be learned about that aspect without acquaintance; hence it is effable, contrary to Nagel's and Jackson's claim regarding phenomenal information. But if there is no dependence, epiphenomenalism follows right there, and as before, "that makes [phenomenal information] very queer, and repugnant to good sense" (Lewis 1990, 514).

I claim, of course, that there is dependence of Mary's behavior on her having learned what it's like to see red, but I also agree with Nagel and Jackson that in one sense (the computational sense) what she has learned is ineffable, or at least cannot be expressed in a public language. So I must blunt the first horn of Lewis's dilemma.

His argument is that, given the dependence, what it's like for Mary to see red can be described as "that on which physical phenomena depend in such-and-such way"—say, as "whichever aspect of her new experience causes her to exclaim, 'So that's what red looks like!'"—and that "this descriptive handle will enable us to give lessons on it to the inexperienced." But this is a very weak sort of effability. No one has denied that facts of "what it's like" can be referred to relationally, e.g., comparatively or in this case causally. All that is denied by Nagel, Jackson, and me is that a subject can specify what it's like to see red or whatever in direct, nonrelational terms.

I may be missing Lewis's point here, for the reply I have just made seems suspiciously obvious. Perhaps, rather, he is tacitly reasoning as follows: If there is dependence, then *some* lessons can be learned about the aspect in question without acquaintance, in terms of the relational description couched in terms of the dependence. If there are other, "intrinsic" lessons that still cannot be learned without acquaintance, then behavior does not depend specifically on this intrinsic information, and so it is epiphenomenal again.

But the preceding conditional is a non sequitur, or at least begs the question against my view of phenomenal information. For on my view, there are intrinsic and ineffable lessons computationally individuated, ineffable because they incorporate distinctively introspective modes of presentation that have no natural-language equivalents, but behavior still does depend on the computational information learned. If it is asked how they can be ineffable in Nagel's and Jackson's sense and still make a causal difference, recall that they are *individuated* causally rather than by truth-maker. Remember the indexical pronouns: "I" is ineffable too.

Strange Qualia

In Chapter 4, I argued that qualitative differences do not out-run intentional differences, the "colors" involved in visual experiences being just the physical colors of represented physical objects, actual or nonactual. But Shoemaker (1982, 1990), Peacocke (1983), and, following them, Block (1990) attempt precisely to distinguish between an experience's intentional content and its more specifically and distinctively "qualitative" content or aspect.[1]

1   SHOEMAKER'S DISTINCTION

The idea is that while two people's visual experiences may be alike in intentional content—the two people are both "seeing redly," being appeared to as by a red object, percep-tually believing that there is something red before them, and disposed to shout "Red!"—the same two people may differ in their intrinsic qualitative color contents; one may be ac-quainted with a green quale rather than a red one. And, as before, their whole population may be split, aggravatedly split and/or kaleidoscopically split, in its spectra. Hence vis-ual experiences have distinctive intrinsic color contents that outrun those experiences' merely intentional color contents.

Thus the already abused term "quale" has grown yet an-other ambiguity.[2] Like me, one can believe in qualia—in introspectible first-order color properties given phenomenally in experience—while insisting that qualia are merely intentional aspects of sensation, represented properties, and rejecting the possibility of aggravatedly split inverted spectrum, as discussed in chapter 4 above, or one can insist that there are not merely qualia in the sense of intentional color contents but also "intrinsic" qualitative contents that outrun the intentional. Hereafter I will call the latter "Strange Qualia" with capital letters.

I have what seems to me a powerful objection to Shoemaker's idea and distinction, as described here (later on, I will examine two other interpretations of his idea).[3] My objection is not fatal, but it poses what I think is a permanent problem for the Strange Qualia view: According to the hypothesis of aggravatedly split inverted spectra and (as I called it) kaleidoscopic inversion, people who see red objects and to whom those objects look red in the intentional sense nonetheless differ diffusely in their Strange Qualia; they (individually) have all sorts of visual Strange Qualia, despite each quale's having been produced in them by a red object and by a process as "normal" as that which produced any of their conspecifics' variously differing Strange Qualia. And all these Strange Qualia are *color* qualia; we think of them as (in some sense) presenting colors to, or being colors for, the apprehending subjects. Moreover, the only way we have of referring to those phenomenal colors is by using our everyday color terms, with a qualifying modifier such as "phenomenal" (I will use "ph-" for short).

So say we have a red physical object surrounded by a crowd of admiring viewers, each of whom is experiencing a different color quale as a result. One viewer perceives ph-greenly, one ph-bluely, one ph-yellowly, etc., and we may equally suppose, one (Fred) perceives ph-redly. But now what does "ph-red" mean? On its face, this usage suggests that Fred has *got it right* and is seeing correctly, while all the other viewers are misperceiving. But by hypothesis, that is not so; this is supposed to be a case of aggravated split. The term "ph-red" bears no closer relation to "red" or to redness than does "ph-green" or "ph-yellow."

The alleged Strange Qualia are collectively a set of properties related to each other as colors are, but now their names are deprived of anything like their ordinary natural-language meanings. Indeed, it is hard to see wherein they are *color* properties at all, for none is red, or green, or yellow, or even a red or green or yellow *analogue,* in the sense of being normally associated with the corresponding physical color.

The point is not just the truism that people do not actually have little color samples in their brains. It is that even the intuitive *picture* or cartoon of people as having such color samples in their sensoria does not help give substance to Shoemaker's and Block's distinction. Indeed, that picture gives the lie to the distinction, since according to it, one viewer's internal color sample (Fred's) does correctly match the red object on display, in that it is ph-red rather than any other ph-color, while the other viewers' samples do not.

To summarize, if (i) there are color Strange Qualia, then (ii) those Strange Qualia are sorted by, or as, or as nonarbitrarily corresponding to, colors. But then, it seems, (iii) to respond to a colored physical object by tokening the corresponding quale is to perceive correctly, and to respond by tokening a different quale is to misperceive. But (iii) contradicts the hypothesis of a kaleidoscopically split inverted spectrum, the tenability of which hypothesis was our only reason for accepting (i), i.e., for believing in color Strange Qualia.

Obviously, this argument extrapolates back from the kaleidoscopic case to the simple, 50-50-split case. It is hardly conclusive, for someone might reject the inference from (ii) to (iii), and I can begin to imagine someone's accepting (i) while denying (ii), but I find both (ii) and the inference to (iii) hard to resist. (In fact, both Block and Shoemaker have assured me in correspondence that (ii) is what they mean to deny, so neither of them falls victim to my general anti-Strange-Qualia argument. However, the resulting view—call it the New Strange theory—strikes me as weird. I will explore it in section 4 below.)

In case I am wrong and there actually could be spectra inverted with respect to the totality of intentional properties, I think there are still ways (available to the functionalist) of modeling such inversion if it should prove necessary. But before documenting this, let me turn to Block's particularly ingenious inversion scenario (1990). What is distinctive about it is that what inverts is not its victim's inner experience but the real physical colors in the victim's environment.[4]

Incidentally, as I noted in note 10 to chapter 4, there is a double relativity to the notion of an inverted spectrum, and it has been widely missed and/or exploited in the literature. We must always ask, *What* is inverted with respect to *what*? The second parameter just expressed (the second "what") has been more salient, though not salient enough: many people grant the possibility of spectrum inversion with respect to (just) behavioral dispositions or input-output relations; less obvious is the possibility of inversion relative to behavioral dispositions *and* underlying functional profile; still less obvious and granted by hardly anyone is the possibility of inversion relative to one's entire molecular constitution. If we are functionalists, our concern will be the second of those three relativized hypotheses, and if we are functionalists, we will not grant the possibility of inversion with respect to one's global functional state (see below). One must be very careful, as many writers are not, to distinguish a spectrum inverted merely with respect to input-output relations from the much more contentious and usually question-begging inversion with respect to global functional state, to say nothing of inversion with respect to global functional state *plus intentional content.*[5]

CHAPTER SIX

Shoemaker's and Block's thesis newly emphasizes the first of the two parameters. It could hardly be spectral qualia in my sense that are alleged to invert with respect to functional state plus intentional content; it is Strange Qualia. And as we will see, there is a third contender as well.

2 BLOCK'S INVERTED EARTH

Here is Block's argument against intentionalizing qualia. He posits an "Inverted Earth," a planet exactly like Earth except that its real physical colors are (somehow) inverted with respect to ours. The Inverted Earthlings' speech sounds just like English, of course, but their intentional contents regarding colors are inverted relative to ours: when they say "red," they mean green, if it is green Inverted objects that correspond to red Earthly objects under the inversion in question, and green things *look* green to them even though they call those things "red." (Let us suppose that there is no split internal to their own population.)

Now, an Earthling victim is chosen by the customary mad scientists, knocked out, fitted with color-inverting lenses, transported to Inverted Earth, and repainted to match that planet's human skin and hair coloring. (Block calls the victim "you.") When you wake up, you experience nothing abnormal, because the inverting lenses cancel out the new planet's color inversion. Your language remains as before, so the natives do not notice anything either. But note that you are now misperceiving; you see green objects as red. You speak falsely, and have false intentional contents. Yet, Block argues, this would change over time:

At first, when you look at the sky, thinking the thought that you would express as "It is as blue as ever," you are expressing the same thought that you would have been expressing yesterday at home, only today you are wrong. . . . Nonetheless, according to me, after enough time has passed on Inverted Earth, your embedding in the physical and linguistic environment of Inverted Earth would dominate, and so your intentional contents would shift so as to be the same as those of the natives. . . . If you were kidnapped at age 15, by the time 50 years have passed, you use "red" to mean green, just as the natives do. Once your intentional contents have inverted, so do your functional states. The state that is now normally caused by blue things is the same state that earlier was normally caused by yellow things. So once 50 years have passed, you and your earlier stage at home would exemplify what I want, namely a case of functional and intentional inversion together with the same qualitative contents—the converse of the [usual] inverted spectrum case. This is enough to refute the functionalist theory of qualitative content and at the same time to establish the intentional/qualitative distinction. (Block 1990, 64)

I have three replies to make to all this. The first reply is only superficial: Block assumes a naive psychosemantics for intentional states, done in terms of "normal causes" or causal "grounding" or both, where these notions are understood more or less statistically. That is, he assumes that when, for a given type of state, a new kind of cause comes to predominate over the state's original normal cause, the state's intentional content actually changes and the state then refers to the new kind of cause.

I reject this psychosemantics. Like Ruth Millikan (1984, 1989), I think of "normal cause" not statistically but teleologically, and I understand teleology in terms of selection history. (A state may have its teleologically normal cause but rarely—possibly never if there is sufficient mismatch between the state's evolutionary origin and its subject's present environment.) Thus, for me, the intentional states of the victim transported to Inverted Earth would *not* change their intentional contents even if that person stayed on Inverted Earth for a very long time and the states ceased having their evolutionarily normal causes altogether.

But the naive psychosemantics is probably inessential to Block's strategy. It would not take much work to construct a variant Inverted Earth case that could be applied, mutatis mutandis, against my etiological psychosemantics.

Here is my reason for saying that: What I think is really at stake here is the general Putnamian issue of "narrow" versus "wide" contents, and biosemantics makes intentional content as wide as does the naive psychosemantics. As I interpret Block's real objection to intentionalizing qualia, it is that *intentional contents are wide, while qualia are narrow.* So let us move right on.

Block's Strange Qualia are very like the "narrow content" allegedly possessed by propositional attitudes. (He almost draws the analogy himself [Block 1990, 69].) Namely, they are *like* the undisputed intentional contents except that they supervene on molecular constitution and so do not shift when the subject's environment is hypothetically or actually rearranged. Generically, my second objection is that any such notion is dubious. "Narrow content" for propositional attitudes is notoriously disputed, often on the grounds that "narrow 'content' isn't content." By analogy, we should suspect any parallel notion of qualitative character, especially when the suspicion is backed by my general argument against Strange Qualia (given in the previous section of this chapter).

But more specifically, Block's argument depends on the assumption, explicitly admitted by him (1990, 66), that qualia supervene on molecular constitution. At least I think that this supervenience assumption is doing some heavy work in shoring up the Inverted Earth example; namely, it nails down Block's claim that despite radical variations in the subject's environment or history or whatever, the subject's qualitative experience remains the same so long as there has been no intrinsic physical change in the subject him- or herself.

Here the dialectic gets slightly tricky: On my own view, qualia (first-order monadic properties of ostensible phenomenal individuals) do not supervene on molecular constitution because they are intentional contents. Block believes there to be Strange Qualia, which outrun intentional contents, and he chooses to add that these Strange Qualia supervene on molecular constitution. (Note that the latter claim *is* additional, even though it figures in motivating the former.) So the question between us is whether there are any Strange Qualia, not whether qualia in my intentional sense supervene on molecular constitution. Block seems to agree that there are nonsupervenient qualia in the sense of intentional contents, so we may distinguish "intentional qualia" from Strange Qualia.

And I see no reason to grant that there are Strange Qualia at all, much less supervenient Strange Qualia. First, I know of nothing that particularly warrants the supervenience claim, and it begs the question against the view that all qualia are intentional qualia: if one is already *assuming* that qualia are nonintentional, "intrinsic" features of sensation, then one will find the supervenience claim plausible; not otherwise. But, second (even if one is leery of adjudicating dialectical charges), there is my general argument against Strange Qualia, in light of which there can be nothing obvious about the Inverted Earth argument at all.[6]

Nonetheless, n.b., we should grant the supervenience claim for the case of bodily sensations, such as pain. For even if such sensations are intentional (as I believe they are [Armstrong 1962, 1968b; Pitcher 1970; Adams 1991]), their intentional objects are parts of the subject's own body, and so molecular duplicates can be supposed to share them. I suspect that this is a major source of the notion that qualia generally are supervenient, for I conjecture that philosophers extrapolate from the supervenience of bodily-sensory qualia to that of colors and other world-perceptual qualia; it is tempting to assimilate the "feels" of perceptual states to those of sensory states, so far as we consider perceptual states to have feels. But the "feel" terminology suits perceptual states less well than it does bodily-sensory states. Bodily sensations are themselves conceived as *feelings,* while perceptual states are not; as Harman (1990) observes, we normally "see right through" perceptual states to external objects and do not even notice that we are *in* perceptual states.[7] Thus, it is fallacious to infer that since bodily qualia supervene on molecular constitution, perceptual qualia do so too.

My third objection to Block's Inverted Earth argument is that one might even concede the existence of Strange Qualia but ramify one's underlying functionalism to account for them. (Remember that my hegemony thesis incorporates an underlying functional profile as well as intentionality.) For example, the comparatively abstract functional roles that underlie intentional responses to colors might be realized at a lower level of functional organization by finer-detail mechanisms, which lower-level mechanisms might differ from person to person; thus if the finer-grained mechanisms' own modest functional roles are narrow, we could identify Strange Qualia with them (waiving my general anti-Strange-Qualia argument for the sake of discussion).

Block anticipates this move, and gives two separate rebuttals. First,

The burden of proof is on the functionalist to tell us what the . . . [narrow] functional states might be. Without some indication of what these functional states would be like we have no reason to believe in such a functional theory of qualia. (Block 1990, 70)

And then,

Perhaps a physiological theory of qualia is possible. If there is a physiological theory of qualia it can be functionalized. . . . Such a move is changing the subject in the context of the inverted spectrum argument, however. Functionalism in that context is linked to the computer model of the mind. The idea is rather as if two machines with different hardware might have different qualia despite computational identity: having the same computational structure and running all the same programs. Since the issue is whether qualia are computational states, you can't legitimately defend a computationalist theory by appealing to the hardware difference itself. (Block 1990, 71)

I am not sure I understand the first rebuttal. What is Block demanding? A description of "what the . . . [narrow] functional states might be . . . [and/or] what the[y] . . . would be like"? But this is an entirely empirical question, hardly to be answered on the spot by a philosopher. Block might as properly ask a type-identity theorist *which* neurophysiological states are the ones to be identified with mental states. If this is indeed Block's demand, it is groundless; if it is not, I cannot tell what the demand is instead.

The second rebuttal concedes that "a physiological theory of qualia . . . can be functionalized." A footnote at just that point cites *Consciousness,* presumably alluding to my doctrine of the "continuity of levels of nature": I deny the existence of any single distinction between "the functional" and "the merely physiological," between "the software" and "the hardware it runs on." Physiological description of brainware is normally itself functional (it contains explicitly and uncontroversially teleological terms, such as "neurotransmitter"). The difference between physiological functional talk and more abstract functional and computational talk is just that, a difference of degree of abstraction and level of functional organization.

Let me elaborate on this a bit, for it will generalize into a functionalist line on inversion hypotheses generally, should we concede the metaphysical tenability of an aggravated split.

3   FUNCTIONALIST INVERTED SPECTRUM

Neither living things nor even computers themselves are split into a purely "structural" level of biological/physiochemical description and any one "abstract" computational level of machine/psychological description. Rather, they are all hierarchically organized at many levels, each level functional with respect to those beneath it but structural or concrete as it realizes those levels above it. This relativity of the functional/structural or software/hardware distinction to one's chosen level of organization has repercussions for each of several issues in recent philosophy of mind, and one must take care not to fall inadvertently into "two-level-ism."

To return to Block's second rebuttal, Block says that my present third move against the Inverted Earth argument "is changing the subject in the context of the inverted spectrum argument, . . . [for] functionalism in that context is linked to the computer model of the mind, . . . [and] since the issue is whether qualia are computational states, you can't legitimately defend a computationalist theory by appealing to the hardware difference itself." But this seems precisely to buy into two-level-ism, as follows.

Suppose that our chosen functionalist proposes to locate ordinary color perception at such and such a level of computational organization, L_n, and accordingly to explicate intentional qualia in terms of L_n. As Block says, the issue is then whether qualia are L_n-computational states. What, then, is the problem? Block seems to be complaining that (a) my move of locating inverted Strange Qualia at a lower level of functional organization, say L_{n-1}, constitutes "appealing to the hardware difference itself" while admitting that the two mutually inverted subjects "[have] . . . the same computational structure and [run] all the same programs," and he seems to think that (b) the appeal and the admission in turn jointly constitute giving up the computationalist-functionalist game (which is, of course, what he wants us to do but not what *we* claim to be doing).

Claim (a) is correct only on a very strictly relativized reading. My move does constitute appealing to a "hardware" difference *if* we are counting every feature of a subject described less abstractly than in terms of level L_n as "hardware." (There is nothing wrong with such relativized usage, so long as one remembers that it is so relativized and that what is "hardware" at L_i is "software" at L_{i-1} being run by the "hardware" described in terms of L_{i-2}.) And my move does constitute admitting that the mutually inverted subjects have the same computational structure modulo L_n. It does *not* admit that the subjects have the same computational structure all the way down. They may differ at the very next level.

For the last reason, (b) is false. By appealing to a lower level of computational organization, I am hardly giving up the computationalist-functionalist game. I am giving up only the very specific doctrine of L_n computationalism.

Block (or someone else) might suggest that the inverted spectrum argument can just be iterated at this point: Having refuted L_n computationalism, we can now use an inversion hypothesis to refute L_{n-1} computationalism, then L_{n-1} computationalism, and so on down. But during this process, the successive inversion hypotheses would become less and less plausible. For example, we would reach the level of neurochemistry, and the relevant inversion hypothesis would have to be that two subjects could be *neurochemically* identical yet experience different Strange Qualia. Block himself, at least, evinces no attraction to any inversion hypothesis of *that* strength.

Granted, if one were to proceed downward through the hierarchy in the way just described, the levels would become less and less aptly described as *computational* at all, even though they would remain biologically functional; it sounds fanciful to speak of individual neurons' computing anything, even though their behavior is still functionally described in the broader biological sense.[8] But this is not to vindicate two-level-ism for the computational. There is still a profuse hierarchy of levels that are computational; and it is unlikely that there is any natural or clear break between the levels that are computational and the next lower level that is not computational but only biologically functional.

Thus Block's second rebuttal, on the interpretation I have given it, simply fails.

4 NEW STRANGE QUALIA

As I have said, both Shoemaker and Block disclaim the theory of Strange Qualia that I have been attacking so far in this chapter. Since I know of no one who has ever held precisely this theory, it must be considered a nearly straw person. My reasons for having discussed it at such length are (1) that it is the view most immediately suggested by Shoemaker's and Block's actual writings, (2) that, accordingly, it may have attracted some adherents from among Shoemaker's and Block's readers, (3) that Peacocke seems to have held a near-version of it, (4) that it is a pitfall to be avoided by any would-be Strange Qualia theorists, and (5) that some of the points I have made in the previous section will carry over to the New Strange theory also.

My understanding of the New theory is based on casual conversation and correspondence, and the theory remains unpublished, so I will not attribute it definitely to Shoemaker or to Block for fear of misrepresenting them. (Each has since changed his position, in any case. Shoemaker no longer defends Strange Qualia at all [Shoemaker 1994a]; Block has renounced the terminology that encouraged the New interpretation [Block 1994, in press, and in correspondence].) But it is worth discussing in any case, for it is a clear and so far unexplored alternative to the view of Strange Qualia trashed in sections 2 and 3.

Let us begin with the denial of (ii), that Strange Qualia are sorted by, or as, colors. On its face, (ii) is reasonable because both Shoemaker and Block use the term "qualia" and because both monger inversion cases: *qualia* strictly so called are the monadic introspected qualitative properties of apparent phenomenal individuals, and subjective color is a paradigm case of such a property, so naturally, when Shoemaker and Block advance inversion hypotheses, we think of phenomenal color properties inverted with respect to physical colors. As we saw, the inversion is also supposed to have been with respect to intentional contents, but the point here is that it is color qualia or Strange Qualia that are supposed to have been inverted, never mind the other term of the relation. (Remember the double relativity of inversion. *Always* remember it.) My problem was that if color qualia or Strange Qualia are sorted by or as colors, the possibility of an aggravated split is apparently forestalled.

But suppose we neologize slightly and think of Strange Qualia not as introspectible first-order color properties but in a higher-order way: we might distinguish an apparent or subjective color itself from the further property of what it is like for the subject to apprehend that color. Such a distinction is already suggested by the apparatus I posited in chapter 3: we describe a quale (in the strict sense) by simply identifying it as a color—say red, as in "a red patch in my visual field"—but if asked what it is like for us to experience that red color, the experience goes ineffable and we are tongue-tied. If the one thing can readily be described in English while the other is ineffable, then it would seem the things are two.

And this would allow for the theoretical possibility that what it is like for me to experience a particular color quale differs from what it is like for you to experience that same color quale; thus an inversion hypothesis. (And the unhappy phrase "what it's like" is now one more way ambiguous, since some people use it simply to designate a color quale.) Further, we might allow that the color qualia with respect to which the what-it's-like-nesses are inverted are exclusively intentional qualia in our sense. Indeed, Block has indicated very clearly that on his view, English color vocabulary always goes with intentional content rather than with Strange Qualia in his sense.[9] The New Strange Qualia, the what-it's-like-nesses, cannot be (noncomparatively) expressed in a public natural language such as English, at least not by the use of color terms. In particular, we cannot use my "ph-" terms such as "ph-yellow" and "ph-red." This is why (ii) is false.

New Strange Qualia, then, are not qualia strictly so called but higher-order properties, and they are not colors in any sense.

I am ambivalent in regard to the New Strange theory. On the one hand, taking it just as I have formulated it, I think it is weird. On the other, I can at need model inverted New Strange Qualia using the apparatus of chapter 3, and so my view will not be threatened even if such inversion is shown to be possible.

Here is why I think New Strange Qualia are weird. New Strange Qualia now do not correspond in any obvious way to colors, for as Berkeley said, the only thing that (closely) resembles a color is a color. So what are they? When people think of qualia generally, the color of a visual sense datum is a paradigm, and when we imagine having our spectrum inverted with respect to whatever, what we are imagining is the inverting of a *spectrum*, i.e., of a bunch of colors. If it is not that, we do not yet know what we are supposed to imagine under the heading of "inverted New Strange Qualia" with respect to the *same* spectrum.

Further, we are told not just that what it is like for me to see a red object might differ from what it is like for you to see one but also that what it is like for me to experience *subjective/phenomenal* red might differ from what it is like for you to experience it. Once the latter modifiers have been italicized, the suggestion becomes hard to interpret, because (I believe) for most philosophical speakers, "subjective/phenomenal red" already names a particular way a sector of one's visual field looks, or what it is like to have that sector look that way. At best, the alleged distinction is elusive.

To be fairer, there is a way of seeing what kind of inversion Block might have had in mind, or at least what kind of distinction. It ties his distinction to effability and ineffability. Again, to enforce the point that it is phenomenal or apparent or subjective color we are talking about, suppose that you and I are confronted by a red object but because of ambient light conditions and/or brain conditions, the object looks green to each of us. Each of us has a green patch in her or his visual field. Now suppose a psychologist (or phenomenologist or anyone else) asks you, "How, exactly, does that patch look to you in regard to color?" You respond, "It looks green." "Yes," says your questioner, "but can you tell me what it's like for the patch to look 'green' to you?" "Um, it looks the same color as that," you say, pointing to an issue of *Linguistics and Philosophy*. "No, I mean can you tell me what it's like intrinsically, not comparatively or otherwise relationally?" "Duhhhhh." In one way, you are able to describe the phenomenal color paradigmatically as "green." But when asked what it's like to experience that green, if you are like most people, you go tongue-tied. So it seems there is a distinction between "what it's like" in the bare sense of phenomenal color that can be described using ordinary color words and "what it's like" to experience a particular phenomenal color, which cannot be described in public natural language at all. That leaves open the apparent possibility that the ineffable "what it's like" might invert with respect to the effable "what it's like." So we have a potential model for Block's inversion. But I am still skeptical about the inversion, if not about the distinction. On the present interpretation, Block is saying, given that each of us (subjectively) has an illusory green patch in his or her visual field, what it's like for you to experience your green patch might differ from what it's like for me to experience my green patch; indeed, it might be just like what it would be like for me to experience a phenomenally red patch. I still have a good deal of trouble with that.[10]

Let me expand a bit on the point about inversion. I believe the New Strange theorist is once again trading on the double relativity of inversion and borrowing intuitive appeal from more familiar inversion hypotheses to lend to this New inversion, which is not intuitive at all: the inversion of *New Strange Qualia* with respect to *the phenomenal color spectrum*. Usually, "the way" something looks is understood in terms of subjective color. The way red things look to me is (what I think of as) (ph-)red. While perhaps under inverted *spectrum* the way red things look to you is (ph-)green, and that Lockean hypothesis makes perfect sense to any twelve-year-old, that is not the inversion hypothesis being offered by the New Strange theorists. (This is a very important point, and it is not only often missed by casual readers of Shoemaker and Block but, in my experience, is a hard one for people to keep in mind even after they have grasped it the first time.) The New Strange theorists have forsaken the "ph-" vocabulary, *which they admit is tied to intentional content,* and so they cannot have that intuitive understanding of switched "ways," and more important, their own inversion hypothesis does not have its usual intuitive authority and pull.

Since the publication of Block 1990, there have emerged two more defenses of Strange Qualia (either original Strange or New Strange—I do not think the difference in conclusion is going to matter to the soundness of the two arguments).[11] One is an interpretation of Block by Robert Stalnaker; the other is a new argument of Block's own.

5   STALNAKER'S VERSION OF BLOCK

Stalnaker (in press) offers an ingenious reworking of Block's Inverted Earth argument that does not rely on the gratuitous assumption that qualitative content must be narrow.[12] It turns on the notion of introspective indistinguishability, which had been invoked but not emphasized by Block (1990). It goes roughly as follows:

(1) For a certain time interval Δt following your transportation to Inverted Earth, your color experiences are introspectively indistinguishable from those that you would have continued to have on Earth. [Conceded all around.]

Therefore, let an *IntInd* property be one such that necessarily, for any two experiences that are introspectively indistinguishable, either both have the property or both lack it. Then,

(2) Throughout Δt, each of your Inverted Earth color experiences e has at least one IntInd property in common with its corresponding Earthly experience. [Seems a safe inference from (1).]

But

(3) During Δt, any given color experience e has changed all its (relevant) representational properties. [According to Block.]

Therefore,

(4) Any such e has an IntInd property P that is distinct from any of e's representational properties. [From (2) and (3).]

So, for all W.G.L. has shown,

(5) P is a Blockian Strange Quale, and so there exist such.

This argument makes no appeal to narrowness per se, even though presumably any IntInd property is narrow. So I must address it on its own terms.

I would make three replies, of which only the third is direct and particularly important. First, an exactly parallel argument can be applied to propositional-attitude contents, showing that your belief that water is H_2O and your Twin's introspectively indistinguishable though false belief that

Twin Water is H_2O must share either a Blockian Strange Quale or a "narrow content" or some further IntInd property. This is an inappropriately short road to a controversial and hotly disputed view, unless the further IntInd property is just a narrow functional property of the attitude in question (such as what Stich [1991] calls a "fat-syntactic" property).

This brings me directly to my second reply to Stalnaker's argument: Since narrow-functional properties can be IntInd properties, (5) hardly follows from (4), because (4) leaves it open that the IntInd property P is just some narrow-functional property of the experience e. And Block has argued independently that his Strange Qualia are not narrow functional properties, because they are not functional. So a new case must be made for the suggestion that (4)'s IntInd property is a Strange Quale rather than a narrow functional property.

My third and most important reply is that we have been given no reason to accept premises (1) and (3) together. More accurately, since (1) must be conceded for at least some time interval, however small, my claim is at least that we have no reason to grant (3) during the conceded interval. And this minimal claim is fairly obvious. After being transported to Inverted Earth, you notice no color difference, introspectively or otherwise, but of course there is also no representational difference at first. The question is whether, as Block contends, a representational difference appears later, but *before* an introspective color difference does. That is, is the interval Δt referred to in Stalnaker's argument large enough to keep (1) and (2) true while falsifying (3), by featuring representational decay prior to introspective color change?

On the Millikanian psychosemantics I favor (Millikan 1984, 1989), representational change would take ages, if it were ever to occur at all; as I said in section 2 above, I do not buy Block's idea that representational change tracks easily with one's decision to speak as the locals do, or with anything else that is tied to public natural languages. If I am right, that is a reason to deny that there is a Δt large enough to keep (1) and (2) true while falsifying (3). But I have volunteered not to make an issue of psychosemantics. And even if Millikan and I are wrong, a further move is available.

Block needs a longish interval during which all the relevant representational contents change but color sensations remain introspectively indistinguishable. Perhaps the representational contents do gradually change, but what shows that the color sensations' Strange Qualia (n.b. again, not the *colors* they involve) do not change with the representational contents? I suspect that a transitivity assumption is at work here: if e_1 is introspectively indistinguishable from e_2 and e_2 is introspectively indistinguishable from e_3, then e_1 is introspectively indistinguishable from e_3, and introspective indistinguishability is maintained over a long interval by way of very short experience-pair intervals.

It will surprise no one to learn that I do not grant any such transitivity principle. First, notice a scope ambiguity in the notion of introspective indistinguishability: introspecting that e_1 and e_2 are not distinguishable versus merely not introspecting that e_1 and e_2 are distinguishable. The latter notion is clearly not transitive; I could fail to introspect a difference between a and b and fail to introspect one between b and c even though I could never have failed to introspect one between a and c. And I doubt that even the stronger notion of introspective indistinguishability is transitive either. The psychologists' concept of a just noticeable difference seems to apply to introspection as firmly as it does to any other form of feature detection, and notoriously, there can be a just noticeable difference between a and c even though there is no just noticeable difference between a and b or between b and c. So we have not yet heard a convincing argument for the claim that the color sensations' Strange Qualia do not change with the representational contents.

One further argument might be that there is no plausible model for such a change in "ways." For example, suppose that the Strange Qualia are supposed to shift from the way blue looks to S at t to the way yellow looks to S at t (remember as always that Strange Qualia are not, and do not correspond to, colors). A shift from the way blue looks to the way yellow looks might reasonably be supposed to be a smooth and gradual shift along the spectrum that passes through green. But it is hardly plausible that you (Block's subject) experience such a shift, and a period of unmistakeable greenness in particular.

I reply that we really have no plausible model for the alleged representational shift either. How does something smoothly go from *meaning blue* to *meaning yellow*? Presumably not by meaning green in between.[13] So my presumed Strange Quale shift is no worse off than the representational shift in this regard; if the present argument works for the former case, it also works for the latter, contrary to hypothesis.

6 BLOCK'S MEMORY ARGUMENT

In my reply to Stalnaker, I suggested that introspective indistinguishability is intransitive and gradually melts away along with (because it is) the representational shift. Block counters this move by appealing to memory: "You remember the color of the sky on your birthday last year, the year before that, ten years before that, and so on, and your long-term memory gives you good reason to think that the phenomenal character of the experience has not changed. . . . Of course, memory *can* go wrong, but why should we suppose that it *must* go wrong here?" (Block, in press).

As Block anticipates, I rejoin by noting the wideness of memory contents, memories being representations. On Block's own view, memory contents will undergo the representational shift. So when you *say* or think to yourself, "Yes, the sky is as blue as it was thirty years ago," you are not expressing the same memory content as you would have when you had just arrived on Inverted Earth. You are now remembering or "remembering" that the sky looked yellow, since for you "blue" now means yellow. And that memory is *false,* since on the long-ago occasion the sky looked blue to you, not yellow. This is my main nonrhetorical answer to Block's rhetorical question of why we should suppose that memory must go wrong here. Not because of anything special about the relation between memory and phenomenal character, but because of Block's own hypothesis of a representational shift: the shift allows introspectively indistinguishable memories to go from true to false.[14]

Though he has anticipated this point, Block does not respond directly. Rather, he adds on my behalf that "since memory is powerless to reveal this shift [in phenomenal character], memory is by its nature defective" (Block, in press). (Call this claim (A).) I agree with (A) as stated, so long as "defective" is understood externalistically and not as implying broken hardware. But then Block seems to take (A), the added remark I have just endorsed, as an argument for my rejoinder to his memory objection. (The dialectic has just gotten very complicated. Block's *memory objection* is an objection to my reply to Stalnaker's indistinguishability argument for Strange Qualia. And now he is taking my remark (A) to be an argument for my reply to the memory objection, which reply was that the memory he cites is a false memory and so cannot be invoked to support introspective indistinguishability.) He says,

But this argument is question-begging. The Inverted Earth argument purports to refute externalist representationism [in Block's new sense, which is roughly the same as my hegemony-of-representation thesis], so trotting in an externalist representationism about memory to defend it is futile. . . . The defender of Lycan's view that memory is defective must blunt or evade the intuitive appeal of the first person point of view to be successful. It is no good to simply invoke the *doctrine* that experience is entirely representational. But the reply to the Inverted Earth argument as I presented it above does just that. It says that the memories of the representation contents are wrong, so the memories of the phenomenal contents are wrong too. (Block, in press; italics in the original)

No, it does not do or say any such thing. But before we get to that, notice carefully that the added and endorsed remark (A) that Block calls question-begging was never an argument of mine against his position or, more to the point, against his memory defense of Stalnaker. My argument against the memory defense invoked only the (generally acknowledged) wideness of memory contents and Block's own stipulations about representational shift, and not in any way the doctrine that experience is entirely representational or any other claim about experience. So the remarks of Block's just quoted fail to bear on anything I have said so far.

In his next paragraph (in press), Block says something that does address my rejoinder to the memory defense (even though he falsely bills it as a way to "dramatize what is question-begging about the argument [namely, (A), which was never an argument of mine]"). He supposes that the protagonist of the Inverted Earth story understands both that his representational contents shift and, philosophically, why they have done so.

But that gives him no reason to back down from his insistence that there is no difference in the way the sky looked to him (in one sense of that phrase), that if he could have both experiences side by side he would not be able to discern a difference. Plainly, he is justified in saying that there is no difference in *something,* something we could call the phenomenal character of the experience of looking at the sky. (Block, in press)

The argument seems to be that the subject is justified in claiming introspective indistinguishability across memories (and hence, presumably, that indistinguishability obtains despite the representational shift). But if the subject does understand both that his representational contents shift and philosophically why they have done so, the subject is *not* justified in saying that there is no difference in memory content. For he would know that his state(-type) that used to represent blue now represents yellow, hence that his own thought that "the sky is still blue" is really the thought that the sky is now yellow, hence that there is a difference despite the *introspective* indistinguishability of the memories. (Remember, Block's present hypothesis is that the subject is philosophically hip; so the subject would already have predicted representational difference despite introspective sameness.) Now, why is he supposed to be justified in thinking that "if he could have both experiences side by side he would not be able to discern a difference," and that "there is no difference in *something,* something we could call the phenomenal character of the experience"?

If anything is doing the justifying, it is surely the subject's memory. But on the standard wide construal of memory content, the memory content has changed and presents a different color, so on that construal the subject's memory would *not* justify him in thinking that the experiences would be indiscernible or that there is a phenomenal "something" that has not changed. Therefore, either Block's argument presumes some *narrow* notion of memory content and that notion accurately tracks a narrow kind of qualitative content, or it simply assumes that the subject has some other kind of access to an unchanging qualitative content over time. But the notion of narrow memory content is controversial all by itself, and that of a narrow and unchanging qualitative content is just the point at issue. So if I have begged the question, I am not alone, and I do not see which assumption of mine it is that does beg.

(Block adds a second argument [in press]; I parenthesize it because I do not follow it. Suppose that Block visits "a different language community in a different country, knowing full well that they cut up the colors differently." And suppose he "resolve[s] to reject . . . [his] old language community and be loyal to the new one" and that psychosemantically this shift of practices changes his representational contents as soon as it occurs. The change, of course, includes his memory contents.

But there is no room here for "gradual" but unnoticed change in what it is like to see red. The externalist view of memory would dictate that my memory of what it was like to see ripe tomatoes just a few moments ago before my decision is wrong. Five minutes ago, before my decision to change loyalties, I was looking at a ripe tomato. Now I have made the decision and I am looking at the same ripe tomato. It looks just the same—as far as I can tell. Yet the externalist about memory has to say that I misremember. [Block, in press]

To the obvious objection, that no such superficial linguistic decision could so quickly change the contents of my standard everyday propositional attitudes, Block replies, "My point is that if anything is wrong with the claim about this thought experiment that the representational contents of my experiences changed in a flash while their phenomenal characters stayed the same, it is this theory of color concepts, not taking memory at face value" [in press].

Having at least tentatively allied myself with Millikan's psychosemantics, I agree that what is most obviously wrong with Block's judgment about this newest example is its guiding theory of color concepts and representational contents generally [either perceptual contents or cognitive-attitude contents]. If I am right, then I do not see the force of the example, since I know of no one who disputes that superficial linguistic decisions and loyalties may change while perceptual and attitude contents remain the same, and I do not see why anyone would doubt that of perceptual contents in particular.

What if Millikan and I are, not just wrong, but as radically wrong as Block suggests, and some mental contents can be changed in a flash by a merely verbal decision? Even then, one may take different lines on perceptual contents and cognitive-attitude contents. Perhaps belief and memory contents might shift, while visual contents remain determined by nature and by the structure and teleology of the visual system, not by verbal decision. That would explain Block's intuition [which I share] that the look of the tomato would remain the same even if belief and memory contents changed. This explanation strikes me as plausible, and it is still representationalist and requires no Strange Qualia. So if I have understood Block's third argument correctly, it fails.[15])

7   BLOCK'S FURTHER ARGUMENTS

Block (1995a, 1995b, in press) offers several more arguments for a thesis that is weaker than the New Strange theory but strong enough to be worth contesting: that what he calls "representationism" is false. Representationism is the claim that "the phenomenal character of an experience does not go beyond its representational content" (in press), and he strives hard against it. Notice that one can deny representationism without embracing Strange Qualia, old or new, for one would be committed only to there being *something* to phenomenal character besides representational content. It might, in particular, be some aspect of functional role, which would be entirely consistent with the hegemony of representation as I defined it in chapter 1. Block further defines "quasi-representationism" as the still weaker claim that "*within* a single [sense] modality, all phenomenal differences are representational differences" (in press).

Now, I am myself a quasi-representationist at best—probably not even quite that—because I have no official reason to deny that *part* of phenomenal character, even within a single sense modality, is constituted by functional rather than representational properties. But in this section I will defend pure representationism against Block's further arguments partly out of *amor belli* and partly out of the conviction that representationism is much more plausible than it appears at first.

Argument 1: Something Overhead

Block (1995b, 234–235) appeals to the difference between a visual experience and an auditory experience as of something overhead. His idea is that each of the experiences is representationally impoverished and has as its (intentional) content only *that there is something overhead,* with not a single further feature predicated. Since the two experiences obviously differ phenomenally, it would follow deductively that some phenomenal character that outruns intentional/representational content.

Like Tye (1995), I think Block is just wrong in supposing that one could hear "something overhead" with no other property ascribed. One cannot hear any sound, even an illusory one, without hearing a certain volume level and some pitch and timbre features. Similarly, presumably the visual experience presents "some ... impression of the thing's size." In his reply to Tye, Block (1995a, 281) concedes the point about sounds, though not the claim about the visual experience, and agrees that the representational difference wrecks his argument. (I think he should have given in on the visual experience also, since even if it does not ascribe size, it would locate the direction and trajectory of the putative object more precisely than the sound could; vision gives far more spatial detail than hearing does.)

But he adds a further argument (1995a, 281):

[T]he loudness of the sound is irrelevant to its representing something as of [*sic*] overhead. The as-of-overheadness of the visual perception seems independent of color, shape, and so on, and likewise for the auditory perception. The difference seems to reside in the phenomenal character of vision as opposed to audition, and that has not been shown to be a representational difference.

That is pretty compressed, and I do not entirely follow it. The irrelevance of the sound's volume to its location does not mitigate the original point that the represented volume distinguishes the auditory experience from the visual one. But perhaps Block means something like this: If you abstract away from the other representational differences, you will still find that the two representations of overheadness itself differ in a kind of qualitative character, one being so *visual* and the other so *auditory*. But if that is the idea, I do not find it convincing. For one thing, I do not know how to introspect a representation of overheadness itself in abstraction from the putative thing's other represented properties, to see if it has some additional qualitative character. For another, Block would need to show that the visualness/auditoriness of the abstracted representations are not simply a matter of their being surrounded by the other represented properties that are being abstracted away from. (In any case, of course, the visual/auditory difference is plainly functional and no threat to quasi-representationism, but I am trying to defend the representationist here.)

Argument 2: Orgasm

Block originally claimed that the phenomenal content of male orgasm is not representational at all (1995b, 234), but has since moderated his thesis, maintaining only that although male orgasm experiences do represent, "there are [phenomenal] features of the experience of orgasm that don't represent anything" (in press; see also 1995a).

I grant, incidentally, that representationism is by no means obvious, as is also illustrated by smells (before one has thought about them) and perhaps even by pains (though I think that pain is a poor example for Block's purpose, since pains not only represent damage or disorder in a body part but do so as one of their main functions[16]). Also, within limits, I accept responsibility for saying what the representational contents really are. My books being family publications, I have not previously investigated male orgasm explicitly, but plausible efforts have been made by Tye (1995, 1996) and Gilman (in press). Certainly the represented properties are ascribed to a region of one's own body (for that reason I have trouble taking seriously Block's suggestion that one might mistakenly attribute one's own orgasm to one's partner). They include at least warmth, squeezing, throbbing, pumping, and voiding. (On some psychosemantics, I suppose, impregnating is represented as well.)

In accepting the burden of articulating representational content, I added the qualification "within limits" because, as Block anticipates, I think it is obviously impracticable to try to capture detailed perceptual and other sensory content in ordinary English words, at least in anything like real time. So the responsibility I accept is just that of giving some plausible general idea of what sorts of things are represented by sensations of this type or that, general but I hope specific enough to remove reasonable suspicion that there are nonintentional qualitative features left over in addition to the functional properties that are already considered characteristic of the sensation.

Argument 3: Phosphenes

Block (in press) claims that phosphene experiences counterexample representationism; "What would the world have to be like for a phosphene experience to be veridical?" Well, there is no denying that phosphene experiences present (usually) colored points of light and larger shapes having some spatial orientation in the subject's visual field. Do they do more than (re)*present* such things? Not that I can see, though I agree with Block that the example settles nothing on its own. I would add (though I know Block will resist this) that the points and shapes are represented as being in external, though dark, physical space; they are not just in the middle of my mind.

Against me, Block urges that "there is no guarantee that phosphene experiences produced by pressure or by electromagnetic stimulation could be produced by light" (in press). Perhaps there is no such *guarantee,* but why does Block doubt that the hypothetically veridical phosphene experiences could be produced by light, e.g., by a psychedelic movie, as I suggested, or by real little lights in an otherwise very dark room?[17]

Argument 4: Bach-y-Rita's Subjects' Tactual Sensations

In Bach-y-Rita's famous experiment, he gave blind people a simulacrum of vision by hooking up a television camera to produce tactual sensations on their backs. Block (in press) observes that the subjects can become aware of the specific sensations on their backs (as such) that are quasi-visually representing external objects, and I agree that if so, the sensations have some mental properties other than their quasi-visual-representational properties. But as a representationist regarding bodily sensations, I hold that what the sensations are additionally doing is just representing the relevant portions of the subjects' *backs* as tingling, mildly perturbed, or whatever. (The sensations represent properties of external objects *by* representing conditions of one's back. I will argue in the next chapter that sensory representation is often layered in this way.)

A character named Marvin (Marvin is a counterpart of Jackson's [1982, 128] Mary)

is raised in a black and white room, never seeing anything of any other color. He learns that fire engines and ripe tomatoes are red, but he never actually sees anything red. Then he is taken outside and shown something red without being told that it is red. . . . He learns what it is like to see red, even though he does not know what that color is *called*. He might say: "So *that's* what it is like to see *that* color. . . ." What does the representationist say about what Marvin has learned? . . . Perhaps the representationist will say ". . . [Marvin] acquires the concept of red without the name 'red'." Perhaps the representationist will say that what Marvin acquires is a recognitional concept . . . that he applies on the basis of vision, even though it doesn't link up to his linguistic color concepts. . . . [But] what, according to the representationist, is the difference between Marvin's concept of red and Marvin's concept of blue? (Block, in press)

Answer: that the former represents the (or a) physical property of objective redness, while the latter represents objective blueness. How those concepts do that, exactly, remains to be settled by a credible psychosemantics, and as I have admitted, I have none of my own. But Block's only objection to the foregoing answer seems to be that Marvin does not know which colors are called, in English, by the words "red" and "blue." I have already rejected the idea that the use of particular English words has much to do with the psychosemantics of *perceptual* representations.

8 PREEMPTIVELY MODELING NEW STRANGE QUALIA

Suppose that representationism is false, that quasi-representationism is false, and even that there are New Strange Qualia. I can handle that if I must. (In section 4 of this chapter I have already displayed one way in which something like a quale might invert relative to one kind of representational content. Here is a second way in which what it's like might invert relative to a quale.) I have insisted on the distinction between a quale strictly so called and a higher-order what-it's-like-ness that emerges only when the relevant subject is aware of the quale. The former is, I maintain, an intentional object. The latter is a perspectival mode of presentation, expressed by a lexeme of Introspectorese that does not translate into any handy natural-language expression. Such modes of presentation, I argued in chapter 3, are matters of internal functional/computational role. So there is at least conceptual room for those to invert with respect to intentional contents: As between different subjects or one subject at different times, the same second-order state might present the same intentional content but play a different functional/computational role.[18] (This would correspond to chapter 5's distinction between coarse factual information and computational information.) It is hardly a secret that functional roles can invert relative to coarsely individuated semantic content (recall the natural-language pronouns discussed in chapters 3 and 5).

(How and why might the internal roles of color sensations differ, given sameness of intentional content? I cannot think of any compelling mechanism or reason offhand, though any science-fiction writer or imaginative Panglossian philosopher might readily come up with one. But equally, there is no compelling reason to think that New Strange Qualia ever really do invert with respect to qualia in the intentional sense, either.)

As before, I do not concede that there is anything of a phenomenal or qualitative nature that supervenes on the brain (except, innocuously, in the case of bodily sensations). That there is would need to be shown. Certainly there is supervenient brain activity that figures systematically in color perception, but it would be neologistic to call whatever that is a "quale," unless it does have the further property of bearing some important, distinctive connection to the *Ur*-notion of a monadic first-order property of an ostensible phenomenal individual.

Thus, in whatever higher-order sense there may be (New) Strange Qualia, those abstract items, pose no threat to materialism, to functionalism in particular, or to the hegemony of representation.

Peacocke (1983) offers three arguments in favor of Strange Qualia, or as he calls them, nonrepresentational sensational properties. As he says, the hegemony of representation or "extreme perceptual theory" implies the "Adequacy Thesis": "that a complete intrinsic characterization of an experience can be given by embedding within an operator like 'it visually appears to the subject that . . .' some complex condition concerning physical objects," or alternatively, that "there are [no] intrinsic features of visual experience which are not captured by representational content" (Peacocke 1983, 10). His arguments are by counterexample to the Adequacy Thesis.

1   THE FIRST ARGUMENT

Here is the first alleged counterexample.

Suppose you are standing on a road which stretches from you to the horizon. There are two trees at the roadside, one a hundred yards from you, the other two hundred. Your experience represents these objects as being of the same physical height and other dimensions; that is, taking your experience at face value you would judge that the trees are roughly the same physical size. . . . Yet there is also some sense in which the nearer tree occupies more of your visual field than the more distant tree. This is as much a feature of your experience itself as is representing the trees as being of the same height. The experience can possess this feature without your having any concept of the feature or of the visual field: you simply enjoy an experience which has the feature. (Peacocke 1983, 12)

This is a striking phenomenon and the argument is impressive. How to respond?[1]

2 LAYERED PERCEPTUAL REPRESENTATION

I think that (like Block) Peacocke here relies on an assumption that can fruitfully be challenged. He supposes that what a visual experience represents is an array of everyday states of affairs involving ordinary physical objects and their standard properties (the road, the trees, the objective sizes of the trees, their relative positions, etc., etc.). This supposition itself is not what I wish to contest, since, of course, the visual experience in question does represent those things. (Or I should say, I agree with Peacocke and Block that it does. Russell would not have agreed that the components of a visual experience represent anything, and possibly not even that the experience itself does.) What Peacocke further seems to assume, and what I do dispute, is that those everyday environmental things are *all* that are represented in vision.

More specifically and at the same time more generally, I want to suggest that a perceptual experience has more than one layer of intentional objects. Indeed, a single apparent color patch in one's visual field represents not just one kind of external object but at least two at the same time. This will take a bit of getting used to.

Let me introduce the idea by switching to a different sense modality, that of smell. In Lycan 1989, I argued that the olfactory perspective is extremely useful in correcting misapprehensions that arise from overattention to vision, since vision is a radically atypical and unrepresentative sense modality. In the same essay I argued—what I grant is not obvious—that olfactory sensations represent. To wit, I claim that a smell actually has semantical properties: reference and a truth and/or satisfaction condition. A smell can be treated formally, *à la* Hintikka (1975), as a function from possible worlds to sets. And it can be given a linguistic-functional "dot" characterization *à la* Sellars (1968), as when he characterizes both the sentence "La neige est blanche" and a pattern of neural firings as ·Snow is white·s. A smell can be incorrect, a *mis*representation. If these perhaps surprising things are true, then surely smells are indeed representations.

And I believe they are true. It may seem that, phenomenally speaking, a smell is just a modification of our consciousness, a qualitative condition or quale or Strange Quale in us, lingering uselessly in the mind without representing anything. Disinclination to think of smells as representations increases when we ask what they might be representing. One might first think that one smell represents natural gas, while another represents roses. The latter is, after all, referred to in English as "the smell *of* a rose." But if the rose smell represented roses, then (a) it would be true or satisfied or correctly tokened only in response to roses, false or incorrect otherwise, (b) it would determine a function that, given a world, determine exactly the set of roses at that world, and/or (c) it would be, in Sellarsian terms, a ·rose·, something that plays an internal functional role analogous to the norm-governed role played by the word "rose" in the public English language. The rose smell does none of those things in humans. In particular, there are objects other than roses that set off the rose smell—artificial rose smells can be made of any substance whose molecules are shaped similarly to those of roses. The point is not that the nose can be fooled. *Au contraire,* it is that in the artificial case, the nose is *not* fooled, and the rose smell is not incorrectly tokened. An artificial rose that produces the rose smell is smelled correctly, for it does have that smell even though it is not a rose. No one would ever suggest that if we discover that other things on other planets smell like roses, the initial categorization of "rose odor" was mistaken. (And conversely, of course, if one experiences the rose smell when presented with an odorless variety of rose, one is not smelling correctly, though it does not follow that one is smelling incorrectly.)

Thus smells do not represent the external things by reference to which they are usually classified, even though they are usually rightly taken by subjects to indicate those external things as well. Nor do phenomenal smells represent, as some Gibsonians would have it, broader ecologically significant properties of things, for the same reason and for others.[2] Thus it is tempting to conclude that smells merely accompany external objects with a fair degree of type-type reliability but do not represent them.

However, there is another candidate for an external representatum. Consider what an *odor* is, in the public sense of the term. It is a vaporous emanation, a diffusing collection of molecules typically given off from a definite physical source. It is itself a determinate physical thing that makes physical contact with the smell receptors in one's olfactory epithelium and sets them to firing. Moreover, there is nothing arcane about this. We are publicly and commonsensically aware of odors; they are public physical entities available for sensing by anyone who, fortunately or unfortunately, happens by. (I am sure each of us can think of our own lovely or loathesome examples.) Now *odor* is a candidate for the representatum, and the idea of an odor as an intentional object of smell resists the objection I have made to the more colloquial candidates. For things other than roses can give off the odor "of roses," and roses can fail to give off that odor. (Again, I am talking not about olfactory deficiencies or misfires but about the match in the physical world between types of objects and types of odors.) Perhaps, then, smells represent odors.

But why think this, even so? Perhaps, to the contrary, all there is to the relation is that smells are highly but imperfectly correlated with odors and that is not enough to make for a case of representing.

Actually, I can think of two positive arguments for awarding representational status to smell, now that the main objection has been circumvented, though I will offer only the first here.[3] It is that once smells are correlated with odors rather than with types of objects, a kind of incorrectness does manifest itself, and hence also a correctness condition or truth condition. If I hallucinate a rose smell in the absence of any rose *or anything else* that is giving off the rose odor, I am misperceiving. The point is not just that my belief that a rose is present is erroneous. I may not even have that belief, knowing full well that my olfactory experience is hallucinatory. Something is perceptually wrong; my olfactory bulb is saying "Rose *odor*" when there is no rose odor physically present, and this report is a lie. Where there is falsehood there is representation.[4]

One may suppose, then, that phenomenal smells represent odors in the sense I have specified. But (in conversation) Ruth Millikan has contended against me that my arguments earlier in this section against the idea that smells represent environmental objects must be flawed. If we are to agree with anything like her pleasantly Panglossian evolutionary-historical psychosemantics (mentioned in chapter 6, section 5), we must suppose that if smells do represent anything, they do after all represent environmental objects of potential adaptive significance. Surely, this is what olfaction is *for,* to signal food, predators, shelter, mates, and other objects of interest ultimately derived from these, and signaling is at least a crude form of representing.

I now think Millikan is right about this, but it does not force me to abandon my claim that smells represent odors. What I suggest is that smells represent adaptively significant environmental entities, and they also represent odors. In fact, they represent the environmental entities *by* representing odors. By smelling a certain familiar odor I also smell— veridically or not—a dog.

Let us return briefly to my original argument against the idea that the rose smell represents roses. It was essentially that if I experience the rose smell when the rose odor is present but no actual rose is, I am smelling correctly, and if I experience the smell when an odorless rose is present, I am not smelling correctly. But in the face of my layered-intentional-objects view, this argument is too simple. For that view (here-after just the "layering thesis") introduces the possibility that a mental representation can have more than one truth value at once. And indeed, I think it is fairly plausible to say that in the first case—that of experiencing the rose smell in the absence of any rose—I am representing *both correctly and incorrectly,* the odor correctly and roses incorrectly.

I do not know how to defend this analysis against the objection, voiced above, that my rose representation is the re-sult of unconscious inference from the olfactory representa-tion rather than being olfactory itself. But this is because philosophy has not resolved the general question of whether the incredibly busy preprocessing that goes on in our percep-tual modules should be counted as unconscious inference (because it is preconscious inference). A clue may be taken from Jerry Fodor's (1983) notion that a module's operation is mandatory and informationally encapsulated. Whether or not such automated perceptual processing counts as "infer-ence" in some legitimate sense of the word, (a) it is not an inference performed *by the subject* in the usual way, but is only something that happens within the subject, (b) it is ut-terly insensitive to other things the subject knows and can use in inference (such as that the Müller-Lyer illusion is an illusion and that the two straight lines with inward and out-ward pointing arrowheads are of just the same length), and most important, (c) the output of a perceptual module unequivocally counts as an object of perception in the ordinary sense of the term (indeed, in listening to human speech we perceive phonemes *rather than* raw vocal sounds, faces rather than geometrical arrangements of particular features, and so on). Thus, even if my rose representation is the result of unconscious inference in one sense, this does not disprove the claim that it is also itself olfactory.

My claim, then, is that a given sensory state typically has not just a single intentional object but two or more arranged hierarchically by the "by" relation. A good model here is that of deferred linguistic reference: By referring to a numeral I refer to a number (and perhaps by doing that I refer to a building, and perhaps by doing that I refer to a government official, all in the same linguistic act—I see no a priori limit on this layering of designata).

Now, how to apply the layering thesis to vision? As we saw, Peacocke seems to assume that everyday environmental things are all that is represented in vision; this is why the Strange Qualia are left over. But the following is a reasonable thing to say: in vision, I see an array of colored shapes, and by seeing these I see a room full of furniture, and perhaps by seeing this I see something still more concept-laden. (In each case, "see" is colloquial for "visually represent.")

As in the case of smell, optical illusions afford at least a weak argument for the layering thesis as applied to vision. Consider first the example of the Ames chair demonstrations.[5] Here is a description of Adelbert Ames's device, by Gombrich:

Most of these demonstrations are arranged in the form of peep shows. One of them which can be fairly successfully illustrated . . . makes use of three peepholes through which we can look with one eye at each of three objects displayed in the distance. Each time the object looks like a tubular chair. But when we go round and look at the three objects from another angle, we discover that only one of them is a chair of normal shape. The right-hand one is really a distorted, skewy object which only assumes the appearance of a chair from the one angle at which we first looked at it; the middle one presents an even greater surprise: it is not even one coherent object but a variety of wires extended in front of a backdrop on which is painted what we took to be the seat of the chair. One of the three chairs we saw was real, the other two illusions. So much is easy to infer from the photograph. What is hard to imagine is the tenacity of the illusion, the hold it maintains on us even after we have been undeceived. We return to the three peepholes and, whether we want it or not, the illusion is there. (1960, 248–249)

A more vivid but still actual example is that of the peep box, which I believe was a toy of the Victorian period in England. It was a more elaborate version of the Ames chair display.[6] A little cabinet roughly the size of a shoe box had a peephole at one end and a light source. When one looked inside through the peephole, one saw a miniature furnished drawing room, in the manner of a doll's house; the furnishings were suitably heavy and ornate. But if one then took off the top of the box and looked directly down on the contents, all one saw was seemingly random little bits of wood and wire and cloth. In fact, those bits had been arranged in precisely just such a way as to present a viewer at the peephole with a perfectly credible but utterly illusory Victorian room.

Now, when one innocently views the contents of a peep box through its peephole, does one see veridically? Here again I think a very proper answer is, "Yes and no." Yes, because one does see shapes and textures that are physically real; there really is a dark red plushy object at two o'clock, for example, even though it is not the sort of object one supposes it is and it may be nearer or farther away from one's eye than one thinks, and one sees real edges, lines, and expanses. But also, no, because one sees a miniature Victorian drawing room that simply does not exist.

Here again one might protest that the room is not perceived but only inferred from what is perceived. But my reply

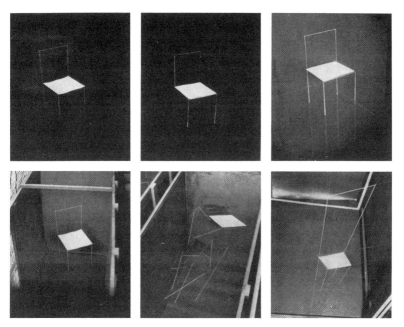

Figure 7.1
The Ames chair demonstrations

would be the same: even if it is "inferred" in some sense, this does not stop it from being seen, an object of the visual experience.

3   REPLY TO THE FIRST ARGUMENT

If all the foregoing is right, then we can answer Peacocke's first argument by denying that the representational content of our visual experience in his tree example is exhausted by the everyday environmental array of road, trees, and background. We do visually represent the trees, and represent them as being of the same size, etc., but we do this *by* representing colored shapes and relations between them. Some of the shapes—in particular those corresponding to the trees—are represented as being larger shapes than others, as occluding others, and so forth. As with all intentional objects, it does not follow that there are any actual things that have such relational properties. And an intentional object is normally "incomplete" in Meinong's way: there are many properties F such that the object is represented neither as having F nor as having F's complement; if the object is nonexistent, it may indeed have neither F nor F's complement.

I am maintaining that the experiential features Peacocke claims to be sensational rather than representational are represented contents after all, though the representata are not physical objects of the everyday sort.[7] But if they are not physical objects of the everyday sort, what are they? What is a "shape" or an "expanse"?

The first important point to note is that shapes, etc., are (represented as being) objects external to oneself, not as mere contents of one's consciousness. When one looks into the peep box, one sees shapes arranged in a certain complex design, but one sees them as residing inside the box, on the other side of the peephole, not in one's own head. They are external things.[8]

The second important point is that not all shapes, etc., are actual. Perhaps some of the edges and lines are actual physical edges and lines seen veridically, for what that is worth, but shapes such as Peacocke's larger and smaller tree shapes do not really exist; in the environment there are no two actual tree-shaped objects, one larger than the other, that we, his protagonists, are observing. (In this way, they differ from the rose odor, in virtue of smelling which we smell the rose itself.)

The third important point is that shapes, etc., are physical, or at least not immaterial. Here, as before, this means that shapes are *represented as being* physical, or at least not immaterial, because they are intentional objects and most of them are intentional inexistents. The shapes one sees in the peep box are visually taken to be physical things of some sort, even if one suspects one is being toyed with and deliberately withholds one's assent to the drawing-room perception. As represented, they may not be very robust physical things. One may think that they are mere facades or that they are flimsy and filmy, or one may not know what to think of them. This is a good case of Meinongian incompleteness. The intentional inexistents are not robustly physical, but they are not nonphysical or immaterial either.[9]

Thus I think shapes, etc., are unobjectionably ill-behaved *intentional objects,* representata. Let us turn, then, to Peacocke's second argument.

4   THE SECOND ARGUMENT

Peacocke's second alleged counterexample goes as follows.

Suppose you look at an array of pieces of furniture with one eye closed. Some of the pieces of furniture may be represented by your experience as being in front of others. Imagine now that you look at the same scene with both eyes. The experience is different. It may be tempting to try to express this difference by saying that some chairs now appear to be in front of others, but this cannot suffice: for the monocular experience also represented certain objects as being in front of others. (Peacocke 1983, 13)

The idea here is in addition to what the first argument was meant to show: Not only do the intrinsic experiential properties or Strange Qualia outrun representational content, but they can vary despite sameness of representational content. The binocular experience differs from the monocular, but not in representational content, since all the front/back relations represented by the binocular experience were already represented by the monocular experience.

But I am not at all convinced. Though offered as an elaboration of the first argument, this second one admits of a special and unrelated reply: Consider the very point of what stereoscopic vision does. When one eye is located at a distance to the left of the other, it sees just slightly further leftward around the side of an object in view, while the right eye sees slightly further rightward around the object's other side. It follows, I think, that the binocular experience contains more information than did the monocular, for one gets a very slightly fuller view of each object that one looks at, even though no new front/back relations are represented. (This observation is hardly new. Hear Joseph Harris's *Treatise on Opticks,* published in 1775: "And by the parallax on account of the distance betwixt our eyes, we can distinguish besides the front, part of the two sides of a near object . . . , and this gives a visible relievo to such objects, which helps greatly to raise or detach them from the plane, on which they lie: Thus, the nose on the face, is the more remarkably raised by our seeing each side of it at once!" [Quoted in Gregory 1986, 156].) For this reason, Peacocke's second argument seems to me to be a nonstarter. (Tye [1992] makes a similar point.)

5   THE THIRD ARGUMENT

Here is Peacocke's third argument for Strange Qualia.

A wire framework in the shape of a cube is viewed with one eye and is seen first with one of its faces in front, the face parallel to this face being seen as behind it, and is then suddenly seen, without any change in the cube or alteration of its position, with that former face now behind the other. The successive experiences have different representational contents. . . . Yet there seems to be some additional level of classification at which the successive experiences fall under the same type. (Peacocke 1983, 16)

Peacocke infers that there is a *non*representational sameness between the two experiences, hence a nonrepresentational or intrinsic feature.

I have two replies to this. First, Peacocke seems to be assuming that in such aspect-seeing examples, informational or representational content tracks with the aspectual conceptualization, and all underlying aspects of the experience in question are nonrepresentational. But that would be far too hasty. Seeing-as is a large subject (Lycan 1971), and I cannot begin to go into the needed subtleties here, but a key point to grasp is that aspectual conceptualization *often* outruns features of experience that are themselves uncontroversially representational. Under suitably rigged circumstances, I can see almost anything as almost anything else. If we are discussing military history and using everyday objects to represent important events, I can come to see a handkerchief as the Battle of Jena.

Perhaps that last example suggests that this is an irrelevantly frivolous use of "see as" and that there is a more strictly visual use. But consider the locus classicus of seeing-as, Jastrow's duck-rabbit figure (known to most philosophers by way of Wittgenstein's *Philosophical Investigations,* part II, section xi). When we look at that figure, we visually represent it as such, though it is then optional whether we take it in turn to picture a duck or a rabbit. Even in this core case, seeing-as is posterior to some visual representation.

Peacocke nearly anticipates this response, agreeing that "something is seen first as a representation of a duck, and then is seen as a representation of a rabbit. But then what is so seen, an arrangement of lines on paper, remains constant in the representational content of the successive experiences. . . . [However,] in the example of the wire cube, this reply is not available: for after the aspect switch, the wires do not all seem to be in the same relative positions as before" (1983, 17).

But now my second reply is that the two cube experiences share some shapes, edges and lines; and, according to me, all those items are visually represented. So there is after all a representational sameness underlying the aspectually different seeing-as experiences; the layering thesis saves the day again, and Peacocke's third argument fails.

6 THREE FURTHER OBJECTIONS

Stalnaker asks what the world would have to be like for the "shape" representations I have ascribed to Peacocke's subject to be veridical, and he questions whether my different-sized tree shapes do visually appear to the observer: "That is not how things *seem* to appear to the observer" (Stalnaker, in press).

I agree that without philosophical training, the observer would not report such an appearance. But I think it remains true that the observer's experience visually *represents* the different-sized shapes. Think of a gigantic peep box that convincingly presents a whole facing environment to the subject by containing large cloths and cutouts and facades arranged in just the right ways. Now recall Hintikka's (1969) and Lewis's (1983a) notion of a *visual alternative,* that is, a possible world logically consistent with the content of one's visual state at a time. There is a visual alternative in which there really are two physical shapes of the sort that appear to Peacocke's subject, one larger than the other, though there are not any actual trees at all. Our huge peep box is one way the world could be in order for my posited shape representations to be veridical, and so this way is one of the observer's visual alternatives and so is a member of the set of worlds that is the propositional content of the experience. (Stalnaker anticipates this point when he offers me the wording, "My visual experience is the way it would be if I were seeing an image (a physical image) that contains two tree images, one bigger than the other" [in press]; just so.)

Tye (in press) makes two objections. First, he tries to convict me of attributing contradictory representations to Peacocke's experience of the two trees. He writes,

For my experience to represent that the one tree shape is larger than the other, it must represent that there are two *objects,* both tree-shaped, one larger than the other. . . . But my experience also represents that those two very objects are trees of the same size. So, my experience represents that there are objects of both the same and different sizes. (Tye, in press)

But I am innocent. I did claim that the experience represents two tree shapes, one larger than the other, and that the shapes (as represented) are physical objects having the relevant shapes. But it does not follow, and I did not claim, that "those two very objects are trees" (Tye, in press), and a fortiori it does not follow that they are trees of the same size. As Tye seemed to grasp earlier on, the shapes are not real, even though they are physical, while the represented trees are real. There are no *actual* tree-shaped physical objects at hand, one larger than the other.

Remember that my model for the layering thesis is that of deferred linguistic reference. To say that I represent a building by representing a number and that I represent the number by representing a numeral is not to say that the numeral is identical to the number is identical to the building. (And if fictionalism holds of numbers, the number in question does not actually exist.)

Thus Tye is both right and wrong in saying, as he does, that the colored-shape layer "is contained within" the ordinary-physical-object layer and that "the levels are not really distinct at all" (in press). Right in that my "shapes" are physical objects in the environment alongside or overlapping the ordinary physical objects there, but wrong in that few of them are identical with any ordinary physical objects.[10]

Tye's second objection is that "the person who looks down the road is not in the grip of *any* sort of illusion" (in press, italics in the original), so I am mistaken in positing a kind of systematic visual misrepresentation, namely, nonveridical representation of the different-sized tree shapes that (unlike the represented trees) do not really exist.

PEACOCKE'S ARGUMENTS

I do not find it so obvious that there is no illusion at all. Recall the giant peep box that I hypothesized in response to Stalnaker. The resulting total experience would in one way be a grand illusion, in that it would present a road and same-sized trees, but in another way it would be perfectly veridical: the shapes would all be real shapes, physical objects of the sort that would appear to the subject to be. Indeed, the subject might know that he or she was looking into a peep box and not seeing a real road and trees. There would be both an entirely veridical presentation and a forehead-smacking illusion, not only at the same time but in the very same experience.

So too, I claim, in Peacocke's example: in the same visual experience there is a veridical presentation of a road and same-sized trees, and there is an illusory presentation of different-sized tree shapes. The experience has one truth condition that would be satisfied by the apparent different-sized shapes and another that is satisfied by the same-sized trees. It happens that the former is actually not satisfied, and in this sense there is an illusion. If Tye thinks there is simply "not . . . *any* sort of illusion" here, he will have to come up with an asymmetry between Peacocke's case and the gigantic-peep-box case to motivate the claim that there is no illusion whatever in the former though there is layered representation and illusion in the latter. N.b., we can grant that the illusion in the peep-box case is in some sense greater, more surprising, outrageous, and authorized by biology and normal visual function, but Tye needs to show that in Peacocke's case there is no illusion whatever, even a tiny, unsurprising, and biologically normal one.

Let me make the same point in a closely related way. Think of introducing undergraduates to Descartes's first *Meditation*. One has to teach them to adopt the first-person perspective, the movie-theater model of the mind. That is a major Gestalt shift, but the students can and do learn to perform it, and then they can also come to introspect their visual experience in abstraction from its normal external-world content. Now if Peacocke's subject were to snap into Cartesian movie-theater mode, she would be obligated by philosophers' trade-union rules to start wondering whether the alleged external world were really there at all. True, she would also have to wonder about the ostensible physical shapes, but intuitively less so than about the richly three-dimensional world of putative ordinary objects; belief in ordinary objects commits one to more. In Cartesian mode, ordinary objects are more likely to be illusory than are mere shapes. But I do not need to make the last point in any very substantive or precise way, for a much weaker one will do: Every ordinary experience admits of a Cartesian Gestalt snap, and so in virtually every ordinary experience, there is a component of shape representation that lets in at least an element of illusion.

I am in no danger of supposing that the debate over the hegemony of representation, Strange Qualia, and nonrepresentational sensational features is finished. There no doubt will be more arguments for Strange Qualia that will have to be answered in their turn. But I have stood at Armageddon and battled for the Lord, and for now the hegemony of representation rages on unchecked.

7   CONCLUSIONS

And since this business so fair is done, let us not leave till all our own be won. I have defended the following claims.

• It is imperative to distinguish all of the very different phenomena and concerns that have been illicitly lumped together under viciously ambiguous terms like "consciousness," "qualia," and "what it's like," and to keep them distinct despite temptation and continuing social pressure to the contrary.

• Conscious awareness is internal monitoring.

• The subjectivity of the mental is real and permanent, but poses no threat to a materialist metaphysics, or to functionalist views of the mind in particular. The same goes for Levine's explanatory gap.

• Qualia in the strict sense are the first-order properties of intentional, represented objects.

• The notion of "inverted spectrum" is doubly and dangerously relative, and functionalism, at least my version of it, is unscathed by any "inverted spectrum" argument.

• Contra Lewis and Nemirow, there is phenomenal information, and Jackson's Mary, the color scientist trapped in a black-and-white laboratory, does learn a new fact in one sense of that word.

• And, of course, the mind has no special properties that are not exhausted by its representational properties, along with or in combination with the functional organization of its components. No sound argument has been presented against that claim, and in particular, no good reason has been given for belief in Strange or New Strange Qualia.

Colin McGinn contends that the mind-body problem cannot be resolved by creatures with minds and bodies like ours, and that although "we know that brains are the de facto causal basis of consciousness, . . . we are cut off by our very cognitive constitution from achieving a conception of that natural property of the brain (or of consciousness) that accounts for the psychophysical link" (1989, 350). I hope that this book has proved him wrong.

Notes

CHAPTER ONE

1
Pace, perhaps, Searle, though what he requires for intentionality is only that a state be "in principle accessible to consciousness" (1992, 156) and/or "potentially conscious" (1992, 173).

2
Actually Block's notion is limned in terms of information flow. The idea is that a significant portion of the information contained in our heads becomes "inferentially promiscuous" in Stich's (1978b) sense, available for reporting, and available for guiding action.

3
For further counterexamples, see Goldman 1994.

4
I thank Georges Rey for urging this remark, as well as for other detailed comments that led me to reorganize this chapter.

5
But see Rosenberg 1986. Also, Robert Van Gulick rightly reminds me that phenomenally, our experience has the property of "being from the perspective of a self," and that as a feature specifically of phenomenal experience, that property sorely needs explaining. Van Gulick himself (1988), Dennett (1991), and Flanagan (1992) have all argued that the perspective-centering "self" should be treated as a virtual entity that emerges from the structure of experience, rather than as being a real distinct observer of the experience. I find their case convincing; Flanagan in particular satisfactorily answers the obvious question of what does the constructing if the perspectival self is only a construct.

6
Sellars argues that the problem is much deeper than this. His argument is formidably complex. I presented a preliminary, simple version in chapter 8 of *Consciousness,* giving some reasons why I am

unconvinced and unlikely to become convinced. I will not try to improve on that discussion here.

7

In saying this, I do not mean to imply that the mosaic is as extensive as we tend to think it is, that it has sharp edges, or even that it is everywhere determinate—all claims that are vigorously attacked by Dennett (1991).

8

Rosenthal (1990a, 1991a) has argued this also.

Assuming that we reject Russellian sense-datum theory, we might say either of two things about the phenomenal properties, such as colors, involved in sensings. One is that they are *not* at bottom first-order properties of individuals, and so are not literally colors of sensings or of brain stuff, but are classificatory. (Nothing in your brain or in your mind is literally *blue* but only of the type "blue." So one must say what it is for a sensory event to be "of the type 'blue'.") Or we might say that the colors are still first-order properties of individuals, but that the individuals in question are not sense data but rather ordinary physical objects, actual or nonactual. Despite their air of mutual competition, I think these strategies are compatible; indeed, I will argue in chapter 4 that both are correct. But the point for now is that on either view, there is no reason why a subject could not be in an unconscious or subconscious color-involving state, and if there is not, then the problem of qualia is neither "the" nor any problem of consciousness.

9

I began the project with respect to subjectivity and qualia respectively in chapters 7 and 8 of *Consciousness*. Parts of it have since also been pursued by Harman (1990), Tye (1994), Shoemaker (1994a), and Dretske (in press).

CHAPTER TWO

1

Locke 1959, book 2, chap. 1, sec. 3, p. 123; Kant 1965, A23/B37, p. 67.

2

There is a potential ambiguity in Armstrong's term "introspective consciousness": if there are attention mechanisms of the sort I have in mind, they may function automatically on their own, or they may be deliberately mobilized by their owners. Perhaps only in the latter case should we speak of introspect*ing*. On this usage, introspective consciousness may or may not be a result of introspecting. Armstrong himself makes a similar distinction between "reflex" introspective awareness and "introspection proper," adding the suggestion that "the latter will normally involve not only introspective awareness of mental states but also introspective awareness of that introspective awareness" (1980, 63).

3
Robert Van Gulick has also written illuminatingly on the uses of consciousness, though he does not focus so specifically on introspection; see particularly Van Gulick 1989, 211–230.

David Rosenthal (in correspondence) has raised the question of why, since integration and control are due to a mental state's causal properties, the state's being conscious would add anything more useful to the causal properties themselves. I would reply that in one trivial sense it does not, since one of the state's causal properties is its capacity to cause second-order representations of itself under the right attention conditions, i.e., to become a conscious state. What its *actually* being conscious adds to its other, more mundane causal powers is precisely that there now exist representations *of* it that can be transmitted in various ways to far-flung parts of the brain and made available to many different subagencies, which could hardly fail to assist integration and control.

4
When I made this point emphatically after a presentation of this material at the NEH Summer Institute on "The Nature of Meaning" (Rutgers University, July 1993), Bill Ramsey responded much as follows: "I see; once you've got the explanandum whittled all the way down, as specific and narrow as you want it, the big news you're bringing us is that what *internal monitoring* really is, at bottom, is . . . internal monitoring!" That characterization is not *far* wrong. Though the doctrine of inner sense is not actually tautologous and faces some objections, I think it is very plausible, once it has been relieved of the extraneous theoretical burden of resolving issues that are not directly related to the conscious/nonconscious distinction per se.

Incidentally, I do not offhand know of any inner-sense proponent who does claim that the theory resolves qualia problems. Yet there is a tendency among its critics to criticize it from that quarter; I conjecture that such critics are themselves confusing issues of awareness with issues of qualitative character. And there is a further instinctive objection to the inner-sense theory that turns on a mistake about qualia (see section 2 of chapter 4).

5
Robert Van Gulick points out (in conversation) that Freud is in one way an embarrassment to the inner-sense view, for if a desire is actively repressed, then it must be the object of internal monitoring of some sort and hence ought precisely to be counted by me as conscious rather than as unconscious. Quite so. To rule this out, I will

need a table of Freudian homuncular organization, a much more detailed notion of "integration and control," or almost certainly both.

6

From a recent trash novel: "Each step was painful, but the pain was not felt. He moved at a controlled jog down the escalators and out of the building" (John Grisham, *The Firm* [New York: Island Books, Dell Publishing, 1991], p. 443. And from a true crime story: "From time to time, she winced slightly as she moved in front of the jury to the easel and back to a stool. For the most part, she was so involved in her intricately constructed argument that she didn't feel the pain" (Ann Rule, *A Rose for Her Grave and Other True Cases* [New York: Pocket Books, 1993], p. 335). I have collected a good many more such examples.

Rosenthal (1991a) offers a nice defense of unfelt pain. See also Palmer 1975 and Nelkin 1989.

7

As has been done by Güven Güzeldere, in correspondence.

8

But see also Sheridan 1969.

9

See Rey 1994 for a more vigorous and more general attack on Dennett's position.

10

See also Dretske 1993, of which more in the next section.

11

Certainly, we should all conscientiously obey Mary Lycan's Maxim, namely, "No *professional philosopher* is qualified to pronounce on the 'folk sense' or 'ordinary use' of any philosophically contentious term (unless the philosopher happens also to be a professional anthropologist and has done the requisite surveys)." None of us gets to kidnap words like "conscious." Perhaps it is time for "conscious" to take its place on Neurath's list of forbidden terms, but I will not urge that as yet.

12

I note that Rosenthal's usage agrees with mine: "Whatever we may discover about consciousness, it is presumably uncontroversial that, if one is wholly unaware of some mental state, that state is not a conscious state" (Rosenthal 1991b, 3).

13

Dretske's nomenclature confuses the issues a bit, for he lumps both Rosenthal's theory and mine under the heading of "inner spotlight" theories, while in the present context he also rightly distinguishes higher-order thought from inner sense and acknowledges that the two are mutual competitors at least in a small way. (See Rosenthal's own objection to inner sense, discussed in section 5 below.)

14

Besides his direct argument against inner sense, Rosenthal deploys an ingenious line of reasoning designed to show that every conscious state is accompanied by a higher-order thought, which, if sound, would support the higher-order-thought theory. Rosenthal might then argue further that inner sense is expendable and should be expended by means of Occam's Razor. His argument is based on the distinction between expressing a thought and reporting a thought and on the claim that all and only conscious states can be reported by their owners; for the record, as I said in chapter 1, I reject the latter claim in each of its two directions.

15

Robert Van Gulick tells me that Kant took "inner sense" to entail a sensuous element. For this reason, my own use of the "inner sense" label may have been misleading.

16

See also Dennett and Kinsbourne 1992a.

17

Kolers and von Grünau 1976; Geldard and Sherrick 1972; Libet 1965, 1985.

18

See, e. g., Baars and Fehling 1992 and Libet 1992. Dennett and Kinsbourne reply to their critics in 1992b. Rey (1994) defends Cartesian materialism on philosophical grounds.

19

For convenience, I will continue to speak of the states that get monitored as "first-order" states, but this is inaccurate, for introspective states can themselves be scanned. This will be important later on.

20

On such distinctions, and for more illuminating examples, see chapters 3 and 4 of *Consciousness*.

21

One might be tempted to infer (something highly congenial to Dennett himself) that introspection is *woefully* fallible, unreliable to the point of uselessness. But this inference would be unjustified. Though the "temporal anomalies" alone should have made us question the reliability of introspective reports, the scope of unreliability exhibited by the anomalies is very small, tied to temporal differences within the tiny intervals involved, a small fraction of a second in each case.

22

Hill 1991 and the present section of this book continue a dialogue begun by Hill 1987 and my response in chapter 6 of *Consciousness*.

23

This likely possibility was called to my attention by Roger Sansom.

24

For a survey and discussion, see Marks 1979.

25

Moreover, as White observes (1987, 168), we have no access to unproblematic examples of consciousness in the absence of self-consciousness, and this fact contributes to an important predicament, which I will expound below.

26

And likewise, White maintains, no notebook computer is self-conscious, even if some are conscious in a less demanding functional sense. (I believe White would accept my claim that mere consciousness is more prevalent than philosophers think [see White 1987, 169].) But I do not see that his analysis of self-consciousness generates this result, since his main concern was to argue only that self-consciousness is restricted to the highest level of organization *in a group organism,* which result does not deny self-consciousness to whole computers. (White has explained in conversation that his analysis alone was not intended to do this; he has other means.)

27

I have defended this thesis before, in Lycan (1985a, 144–145).

I should note that Searle himself goes on to qualify his "on/off" claim: "But once conscious, the system is a rheostat: there are different degrees of consciousness"; he speaks of levels of intensity and vividness (1992, 83). Thus, it seems, our real disagreement is over, not degrees *per se,* but the question of whether a creature or device could have a much lower degree of consciousness than is ordinarily enjoyed by human beings and still qualify as being conscious at all.

28

Incidentally, I do not mean to deny even that an individual state/ event's being a conscious one is similarly a matter of degree. Kirk (1994, 156) and Ned Block (in correspondence) have pointed out that we have experiences that are conscious to some extent, even though we pay scant heed to them. That is exactly so, on my view; there are of course degrees of attending.

29

I should emphasize again that a monitor makes for consciousness when *what* it monitors is itself a psychological state or event. My suggestion that notebook computers are after all conscious is con-

167

ditional on the highly controversial assumption that such computers have psychological states such as beliefs and desires in the first
place.

30

By way of further diagnosis Rey (1983, 25) offers the additional
conjecture that our *moral* concern for our living, breathing conspecifics drives us to posit some solid metaphysical difference between
ourselves and mere artifacts as a ground of this concern. He opines
that we need no such ground in order to care more for human beings
than for functionally similar machines, but he does not say what he
thinks *would* ground this difference in care.

Rey has reworked his original paper, and the new version
(1988) contains a number of important improvements, though I do
not see that any of them bears on my rebuttal here.

31

Joe Levine has raised a question similar to that of David Rosenthal's
addressed in note 3 of this chapter: he asks rhetorically whether, if
a block were inserted in my brain so that the representations I have
mentioned could not get out to motor systems and the like, this
would make me "less conscious." I reply that this very much depends on where the block is inserted. If it is fairly peripheral and
merely blocks signals to the motor systems themselves, paralyzing
me to some degree, then I would not say that it would lower my degree of consciousness very much, though, as has been argued by
Johnson (1987), Rollins (1989), and others, the interaction of mental representations with motor skills has been underappreciated,
and restraints on motor function may lead more directly than we
might expect to diminution of mental capacities. If the block
is fairly close to the source first-order states so that none of the
second-order representations gets very far or reaches any signifi-
cantly different and distant cognitive or conative subagency, then,
yes, I should expect that in the relevant respect this would make me
less fully conscious. And, of course, there are possibilities in
between.

32

Samuel Butler said, "Even the potato, rotting in its dank cellar, has
a certain low cunning." But I grant the potato has no internal
monitors.

I fear that some readers will want to offer a competing explanation of the imaginative predicament I have noted: that the reason
we cannot imagine the tiny consciousness of a spider or that of a
notebook computer is that there is "nothing it's like" to be either of
them. On the pernicious explanatory uselessness of the "what it's
like" locution, see chapters 4 and 5.

168

33

This is the one argument I gave in Lycan 1985a. Notice carefully that although it and the others offered here take slippery slopes as their major premises, they are not slippery-slope arguments in the pejorative sense. For they do not argue from categorical facts at one end of the slope ("Kojak is bald" or "Infanticide is wrong") to the corresponding categorical judgments at the other end ("Everyone is bald, no matter how much hair they have" or "Contraception is wrong"). On the contrary, they argue that the concept in question is not a sharp-edged concept but comes in degrees.

Some related points are made by Kirk (1994, section 5.9).

34

"I have no idea whether fleas, grasshoppers, crabs, or snails are conscious" (Searle 1992, 74). He suggests that neurophysiologists might find out, by a method of apparent-consciousness debunking, namely, looking for evidence of "mechanical-like tropisms to account for apparently goal-directed behavior in organisms that lacked consciousness" (1992, 75); he pooh-poohs "mechanical-like" functional processing as being in no way mental or psychological. On this, see Dennett 1993.

Searle offers an objection of his own to the "inner sense" model of conscious awareness:

> Where conscious subjectivity is concerned, there is no distinction between the observation and the thing observed, between the perception and the object perceived. The model of vision works on the presupposition that there is a distinction between the thing seen and the seeing of it. But for "introspection" there is simply no way to make this separation. Any introspection I have of my own conscious state is itself that conscious state. (1992, 97)

But, not surprisingly, I do not grant the premise, nor do I see why Searle accepts it. If at a given time I am in a first-order psychological state of which I am unaware and then (for whatever reason) I focus my internal attention on the relevant phenomenal field and thereby become aware of the first-order state, the state becomes a conscious state, for introspecting has made it so. But the introspection I have of the state is not "itself that conscious state"; it is a superadded attending, having the state as its intentional object. By hypothesis, the state existed before any introspecting was done, and awareness made it a conscious state, so the introspecting could hardly be identical to the state itself.

35

He reasonably questions whether the particular continua I have mentioned—the phylogenetic scale, infant development, and so on—are indeed rightly characterized in my terms as continua of increasingly rich and effective internal monitoring. Though, of course, it is my thesis that they are, I grant that my notion of "rich and effective" is little more than a placeholder, and that my analysans "has more monitors, monitors more, integrates more, integrates better, integrates more efficiently for control purposes, and/ or whatever" may only set off a chisholming process of counterexample and refinement. (Since this book went to press, Tom Senor has begun the chisholming, and I have begun the refinement.)

CHAPTER THREE

1
Completely, of course, only relative to a chosen level of nature. As we all know, this notion of completeness relative to a level needs a good bit of spelling out, but the spelling out would be pretty routine business.

2
The question of "what it is like to be a bat," the concern behind it, and moreover a powerful response to that concern go back at least to Farrell 1950. The concern, minus only the "what it's like" locution itself, is found in Broad 1925, 71–72.

3
Namely, (G) and (H) from chapter 1. In *Consciousness* I did not consider (K) and (L).

4
Note too Douglas Hofstadter's remarks about the intended "subjectlessness" of Farrell's, Nagel's, and Jackson's "what it's like" locution (Hofstadter and Dennett 1981, 406 ff.). In the only *plain* sense of "subjectless," there is something it is like to be anything, even a cardboard carton or a bunch of McDonald's french fries. What is it like to be a bunch of french fries? Take a look at any bunch of french fries and you will see what it is like for something to be one.

As we will see in chapter 5, there is a further distinction to be made between philosophical senses of the phrase "what it's like," which bears directly on the ontological analysis of sensory experience.

5
There are, of course, finer-grained ways of individuating "facts." I address this point below.

Chapter 7 of *Consciousness* examined the "knowledge argument" in very much more detail and argued that besides the apparent Leibniz's Law fallacy, Nagel has bought into private ostensive definition, as bashed by Dewey, Wittgenstein, and others. Nagel has been widely criticized in the literature on these and numerous other points by, e.g., Hofstadter and Dennett (1981), Rosenthal (1983), Nemirow (1990), Lewis (1990), Van Gulick (1982), Churchland (1985), Levin (1986), Tye (1986), Marras (1993), and many others. Jackson is scouted by Horgan (1984) and, quite differently, by Dennett (1991). Various rejoinders and diffuse commentaries have ensued, but it seems to me that *all* the critics' initial complaints are sound.

I should note that Nagel is not pushing Cartesian spookstuff, even though he thinks he has found science-resistant funny facts and/or funny properties. Elsewhere he takes pains to grant that "there is just as much difficulty in understanding how [a Cartesian soul] could have a point of view" (Nagel 1979, 190).

6
This argument is developed at more length in *Consciousness,* chap. 7, sec. 4.

7
McClamrock (1995, 172–173) offers a well-aimed criticism, in sum that "if the sense in which the 'function' is objectively describable is just that *anybody constituted in the right way* can characterize it, then no rebuttal has been given to the claim that no objective theory can characterize the facts about bat phenomenology so that they can be referred to by beings (like us) who don't share the bat's structure and perspective." It is true that beings like us cannot use the characterizations in terms of functions from possible worlds, and I think McClamrock's point is effective against my present way of formulating the argument. But note that the limitation on us is due to our finitude and lack of Godlike ability to survey nondenumerabilities of nondenumerabilities of possible worlds, not in particular to our not being bats.

8
In previous writings, Nagel has explicitly shown himself to know better, e.g., 1965, pp. 341 ff. No doubt he is still well aware of the fact. But the slip is not surprising; we all make it now and again if we are not careful. That is why I gave it a special name. In chapters 2, 7, and 8 of *Consciousness* I documented any number of its other instances in the writings of well-respected philosophers of mind. It is, I think, one of the leading causes of "qualia" sickness.

Incidentally, my use of the label "Banana Peel" in *Consciousness* may not have been entirely clear, for some commentators have mistaken its reference; e.g., Kobes renders it as "[the assumption] that there are phenomenal individuals. On this assumption there are such things as pains and after-images which have such properties as painfulness and greenness" (1991, 153). But it is too bald to call the Banana Peel an "assumption." Nagel does, and Kripke probably would, explicitly disavow that assumption, though (I claim) each has slipped on the Peel, and Frank Jackson explicitly defends it, but is *not* a Peel victim. Rather, one slips on the Banana Peel when, while disavowing phenomenal individuals, one appeals to a premise that is plausible only so long as one is tacitly thinking in terms of phenomenal individuals. (A small distinction, I agree. Does the Peel victim, then, not *tacitly assume* the existence of phenomenal individuals even though overtly denying it? Perhaps, in a suitably remote sense of "tacit," but I would rather officially back off from this accusation. In any case, "Banana Peel" has never been the name of the phenomenal-individual thesis itself.)

9
See chapter 8 of *Consciousness,* where I maintain that phenomenal properties are real and must be taken as properties of individuals. (I argue that we would do better to take the individuals in question to be nonactual physical objects rather than actual phenomenal ones, but I can sympathize with anyone who might not share this preference.) This view will be developed further in chapter 4 below.

10
Over the years a number of people, including Derek Browne, Jack Copeland, and Bob Van Gulick, have suggested to me that there is room for a physicalist notion of a phenomenal object, and so I should not simply assume that phenomenal objects are nonphysical. Indeed, Kobes (1991) has begun trying to work out this suggestion. I do not reject it out of hand, but I am not yet convinced that good sense can be made of it.

11
On the specifically epistemological significance of points of view and the scientific urge to abstract away from them, see Rosenthal 1983.

12
For discussion of the immense literature on that issue, see Boër and Lycan 1980; 1986, chapter 6. The connection between the issue and Nagel's knowledge argument is made in Boër and Lycan 1980, 446 n., 450 n., and in *Consciousness,* chapter 7, section 6. It is also proclaimed and ingeniously elaborated by McGinn, who argues, "Our *faculties* may be such as to make it necessary that things be represented as having certain properties without it following that those properties are possessed by things objectively or intrinsically" (1983, 93). McMullen (1985) spells out the connection between Castañeda's and Nagel's arguments more specifically. McMullen's common denominator is that in each case an indexically or demonstratively expressed thought can be fully understood only by someone occupying the right point of view. Her line on this common

feature is to distinguish descriptive psychological associations from semantic value and to hold that understanding involves the former as well as the latter. I think this is crucially right (see Lycan 1985b). McGinn, McMullen, and I all take the view that "subjective," perspectival, indexical states of subjects are a matter of *combining* a represented "objective" state of affairs with a distinctive mode of representation, which mode of representation cannot, or could not normally, be used by any other subject to represent the very same state of affairs, as opposed to a corresponding one like it, though the represented state of affairs is as it is apart from any of the various modes of representation (see below).

13
In what follows, I will merely summarize the view I have developed in some previous works, particularly Lycan 1981, 1985b, 1987, and Boër and Lycan 1986. For an excellent critical discussion of the theory defended in those works, see Tomberlin 1990.

14
This commonsensical view is, of course, controversial on each of several fronts. But I have defended it at length elsewhere, particularly in Lycan 1988.

15
"Dthis" cannot be replaced in any sentence ("Dthis has five letters," "Dthis is a pronoun," etc.) by any term that does not both designate the same word and designate it in the same computational way. Though no natural language contains "dthis," any natural language might do so. The list of examples could go on and on.

16
The hypothesis I am about to propose has also been suggested independently by Leeds (1993) and by Rey (1991), though Rey (1992a) defends a different view, in that Rey seems to have shifted his allegiance to the competing theory defended by Nemirow (1990) and Lewis (1990). Loar (1990) takes a related view and defends it in a way that is quite congenial to mine.

17
I do not mean to claim that all the outputs of the internal scanners must be primitive rather than composite. Indeed, it might empirically turn out that all the outputs are composite. But then I would make the same claims as I am making in this section about the outputs' primitive components, and the same explanation would go through.

Nor am I contending that the introspector outputs would be *logically* private in the sense impugned by Dewey and Wittgenstein. Logically speaking, another person could be syntactically/inferentially/conceptually privy to my first-order state in the way that I am if that person were futuristically wired into my first-order brain in the way that he is by nature wired into his own first-order brain.

Thus he could introspect a psychological state of mine by means of a syntactically similar representation; he would think of the introspected state as his own. But this will never happen in the real world.

18
This concern was articulated for me by Robert Van Gulick.

19
However, I would insist that an English expression might well be logically equivalent and even intensionally isomorphic to the bat's introspective word. The possible-worlds argument of section 2 above shows this.

20
Levin (1986) also emphasizes the independence of the alien-concept issue from the matter of factual knowledge. McMullen offers a related example: "An English speaker who doesn't know French finds herself on a street corner in Paris and asks a Parisian passerby for directions to the Metro. The fact that she cannot use the information in the inevitably French response does not show that English directions represent something that the directions in French do not" (1985, 229). The only difference between McMullen's English speaker and human speakers confronting the bat is that a human speaker has the conceptual potential to learn French but does not have the conceptual potential to learn Bat Mentalese.

Pereboom (1994) contends that my analysis has only put off Nagel's and Jackson's problem, for that problem recurs at the level of second-order representing. Consider the state of *introspecting* one's state of sensing red.

> If materialism is true, exhaustive factual knowledge of this further state, a state which features the typical human phenomenological mode of presentation of *sensing red—what it is like to sense red*—will be had by someone who has complete physical knowledge but has never enjoyed a sensation of red. But, the anti-materialist should object, it will not be. Just by having the complete physical knowledge one will not know, for example, that
>
> (1)   The mental state that features the typical human phenomenal mode of presentation of *sensing red* has *this* property,
>
> where "*this*" refers to what it is like to sense red.
>
> This objection captures all of the original force of Nagel's and Jackson's arguments. (1994, 324)

I agree that it does, since I do not think those arguments have much force; presumably what Pereboom means is that it has *more* force in that it does not admit of my sort of reply. But unless I am missing Pereboom's point, the objection is susceptible to my treatment. Of course, one who has not sensed red cannot know (1) as it is formulated. But what fact (in my coarse-grained sense) does (1) describe? What is it for the mental state that features the typical human phenomenal mode of presentation of sensing red to have "*this*" property? The property is not redness but a higher-order classificatory property expressed in Introspectorese. And that is just, scientifically speaking, for the complex mental state to consist in part of a monitoring of the first-order red sensing, which monitoring has a distinctive functional/syntactic profile. As always, one can know that fact under its scientific mode of presentation without knowing it in its introspective guise.

21

Much the same point is raised and combatted by Kirk (1994, chap. 7).

22

Thus I agree with Searle that "there is no way I can observe someone else's consciousness as such; rather, what I observe is him and his behavior and the relations between him, the behavior, the structure, and the environment" (1992, 97). But I would add that the subject's consciousness (in whatever sense) just is some subsegment of the relations between him, the behavior, the structure, and the environment, even though to observe it/them from the outside is not to observe the consciousness *as such*.

23

In the originally published article on which this chapter is based, I called the property "wooziness," but I found that this term confused readers by suggesting that the property was somehow mental. It is important to see that blutsiness is in no way mental but is a physical aesthetic feature of the painting that K. happens to be able to detect.

24

There is at least one sense in which an explanation could be given: the good old classical Hempel and Oppenheim deductive-nomological sense. That is, the art critic might form a lawlike generalization correlating instances of blutsiness with K.'s perceivings as of blutsiness as manifested by his avowals, and a psychophysiologist might even arrive at finer generalizations governing the ways in which this correlation is mediated by K.'s brain mechanisms. In this way, all K.'s blutsiness reactions could be pre- or retrodicted, and so explained in the deductive-nomological sense. But the same is true of our own sensations, the bat's sonar sensation, and all other sensations; if mere deductive-nomological "explanation" is in question, there is never a principled explanatory gap.

25

In their Introduction to Davies and Humphreys 1992, the editors maintain that there is "one clear divide" between "the optimists about explanation" and the "mysterians" (Flanagan's [1992] term), such as McGinn (1989), who insist that the mind-body problem is insoluble on account of subjectivity (Davies and Humphreys 1992, 34). Ahem. I do not think the divide Davies and Humphreys mention is *entirely* clear, because my own position is neither purely optimistic nor mysterian. For the reasons given in this chapter, I believe in Levine's (1983) explanatory gap and that the gap is probably permanently unbridgeable. But I am no mysterian, for I argue that the gap's existence is neatly predicted, explained, and rendered harmless by my own entirely nonmysterian theories of conscious awareness and subjectivity; the mind-body problem is solved, at least till someone comes up with a further difficulty.

26
Following Armstrong (1961, 1962), Pitcher (1970, 1971), and Adams (1991), I would claim that *all* sensation represents. Representata include both states of the physical environment and internal, typically damaged or disturbed, states of one's own body. (More on this in chapter 6.)

27
Nemirow (1980, 1990) and Lewis (1990) suggest that whatever is distinctive about "knowing what it is like" is a matter of a skill or aptitude, a "knowing how" rather than a "knowing that." Insofar as knowing how is a functional condition, I would agree that knowing what it's like involves a knowing how, but I agree with Jackson against Nemirow and Lewis that it is also a knowing that (see chapter 5 below).

28
This is emphasized by Perry (1979).

29
One concession: In my view, the knowledge argument does refute the doctrine that Jackson somewhat misleadingly calls "physicalism," namely, that "all (correct) information is physical information" (1982, 127), when this is understood as a claim about *truths* rather than about what there is. (Flanagan [1992, 98] calls this "linguistic physicalism.") Unlike Nemirow and Lewis, I grant that there are truths that cannot be stated in any language of science (see chapter 6). But this is a linguistic doctrine, not an ontological one.

CHAPTER FOUR

1
Actually the term "quale" predates Lewis; it was used, though less precisely, by Peirce (1931/1898).

2
One need not endorse a Russellian sense-datum metaphysics or epistemology in order to use the term "quale" in this way; just think

of the color that suffuses a particular subregion of one's visual field at such and such a time.

3

Laudably, there have been other attempts to use "quale" more specifically. Owen Flanagan proposes to define it thus: "A quale is a mental event or state that has, among its properties, the property that there is something it is like to be in it" (1992, 64). But (1) it seems peculiar to say that an event of afterimaging *is* a quale, rather than that it presents (or features or involves) one. And (2) as we have seen in chapter 3 and shall see much more vividly in chapter 6, the phrase "what it's like" is more sinning than sinned against; nothing whatever is clarified or explained by reference to it, and it itself is not only badly in need of explanation, in general, but is also ambiguous in at least three ways, in particular.

Ned Block (1990, 1994, 1995b) creates more than one culpable further neologism of "quale," and he occasionally equivocates between them. He begins Block 1994 by talking of "ways it feels" and "experiential properties of sensations." By that he could mean qualia in the strict sense, but later it becomes clear that he does not. He wants to define the term so that the existence of "qualia" is controversial. And he says, "Opponents of qualia think that the content of experience is intentional content . . . , or that experiences are functionally definable" (1994, 514), so he defines qualia contentiously: "Qualia are experiential properties of sensations [etc., that] are not intentional or functional or purely cognitive."

I object strongly to this, because I think of myself as a staunch defender of qualia, and in what is a perfectly good sense of the term, as well as being the (nearly) original sense. Also, I have opponents myself: all the adverbialists, Dennett, and Wittgensteinians, for example. But let us look more closely at Block's notion.

His definition runs together two issues better kept apart: "representationism" as Block calls it (the doctrine that all the qualitative content of experience is intentional or representational content), and functionalism in whatever form. A nonfunctionalist could hold representationism, and many philosophers are functionalists but reject representationism. Thus there are two weaker notions of "qualia": *nonintentional qualia* are "experiential properties of sensations [etc., that] are not intentional . . . or purely cognitive," while *nonfunctional qualia* are "experiential properties of sensations [etc., that] are . . . not functional or purely cognitive." Block used just the first of those senses in Block 1990; the stronger, mixed notion did not appear until Block 1994.

But as we will see in chapter 6, to our cost, there is a remaining interpretive issue. A quale in the strict sense is a first-order property, such as a color. And for all Block had said in print until very recently, his "qualia" are first-order properties too. But in Block, in press, and in recent presentations and conversation, Block now casts his "qualia" as *higher-order* properties involved in sensation. In particular, and oddly, visual "qualia" are not color properties. As of 1996, Block's "qualia" are *higher-order relational experiential properties of sensations (etc.) that are not intentional or functional or purely cognitive.*

I think that wanton neologism, especially of what was a defined technical term to begin with, should carry a prison sentence.

4

In correspondence, Robert Van Gulick has asked how, then, such a thing can be an object of perceptual awareness in and at our own world. It does sound odd to speak of our perceiving a physical object that inhabits not our own world but a different, causally unconnected one. But remember that "perceive" is not being used as a success verb here; my claim is only that the alien objects are *visually represented*, and representations can be false and portray nonexistent things.

5

See especially Campbell (1969), Hilbert (1987), and Hardin (1988).

6

For its best statement, see Armstrong and Malcolm 1984, 170–182; see also Armstrong 1987. A similar view is taken by Jackson and Pargetter (1987).

7

Hilbert (1987) defends a similar view, but with an added realist twist.

8

At least early on, Armstrong himself was more optimistic; see, e.g., Armstrong 1968b, 288–289. He had an ulterior motive for this optimism: his conservative views on what properties count as genuine universals and his doubt that there are any properties that are not genuine universals (see Armstrong 1978).

9

Again, Rosenthal (1990a, 1991a) makes a similar point.

Against my version of Armstrong's appeal to the long-distance truck driver, Block attempts to show that the driver does actually experience the redness of the lights, etc.:

> Nissan is funding some work at MIT that apparently includes an investigation of this phenomenon, and I have been told some simple preliminary results. If you probe "unconscious" drivers, what you find is that they can always recall (accurately) the road, decisions, perception, and so on, for the prior 30–45 seconds, but farther back than that it's all a blank. . . . This

seems a clear case of experience as genuine as any but quickly forgotten, a moving window of memory. (1995a, 280)

Now, this may be verbal, since in chapter 2, I did not mean to be dogmatic in suggesting that monitoring is necessary for what most people would call "experience," and I am perfectly willing to grant a weaker sense of "experience" in which the driver subconsciously experiences the redness, etc. (compare my two senses of "pain").

But I doubt that the disagreement is merely verbal. I suspect that Block thinks that the experiences are not subconscious at all, even though the driver is not especially *attending* to them. Perhaps the driver is passively aware of experiencing the redness, etc., though only dimly.

I do not think so, but more to the point, Block's *argumentum ad Nissanum* fails to show that. Even if it is true that when a driver is probed in midreverie, he can recall perceptions of the road from the previous thirty seconds, that does not show that the driver *was* to any degree aware of the perceivings back at the previous time. There is no inconsistency in saying that (1) at t_1 the driver perceived the redness, (2) the driver, being distracted, was entirely unaware of doing so, yet (3) at t_2 the driver is probed and is then able to access memories of the perceivings, those memories being traces left by the earlier perceivings despite their having been subconscious.

10

It is important to notice a *double* relativity in the concept of an inverted spectrum: an inversion hypothesis is stronger or weaker, depending on the features of a subject modulo which the spectrum is said to be inverted, and there is even some variation in the "spectrum" that is supposed to be inverted (see chapter 6). In this section I am concerned with inversion of color qualia with respect to environmental visual stimuli, not, e.g., with "inverted qualia" objections to functionalism.

11

Lycan 1973, scooped by Gert (1965) and Taylor (1966). See also Shoemaker 1982.

12

Point (2) may be very old, but so far as I am aware, it was first made by Charlie Martin in conversation with Armstrong.

13

Following Shoemaker (1982), Block (1990) concedes a sense in which red objects still "look red" to an inverted-spectrum victim in whom they actually produce green-type sensations. The subject uses color words in the same way as do members of her speech community and also internally classifies experiences according to the same scheme. Hence she can be described as *believing* that red objects are red and as perceiving them as red. This alleged distinction between senses of "looks red" will be addressed in chapter 6.

14

Armstrong was once tempted by this (1968b, 258).

15

See especially Harrison 1973, 102–114. Harrison's argument is criticized by Shoemaker (1982) and by Hardin (1988, 142 ff.), though Hardin goes on to supply different arguments in support of Harrison's conclusion.

16

Notice in any case that (3) does not follow from (2). A split may be even (50-50) without being an aggravated split, so long as it results from some asymmetrical normal/abnormal disparity. And the very tough line *is* very tough only so long as we are assuming symmetry.

17

This does not, of course, entail that for an individual organism to have a color experience, it must be surrounded by an actual population of conspecifics. The last remaining member of a species still exhibits a normal/abnormal distinction, in virtue of its genetic and evolutionary heritage. Thanks to Georges Rey for insisting on this clarification.

18

A circumstance that has caused almost as much trouble in metaphysics as the wild imaginations.

My point about imaginability is elaborated by Horgan (1987, sec. III).

19

See Hart (1988, chapters 2 and 3).

20

Ned Block (1990, 59 and n. 15) seems to reject this methodological idea, for he complains of Harman's and my having dismissed his original inverted-spectrum argument (Block 1978, reprised from Block and Fodor 1972) in this same way. But the dialectic here is complicated, for he distinguishes his present inverted-spectrum argument from a simpler "straw" inverted-spectrum argument, which he pooh-poohs and which he grants is refuted by my methodological argument. The trouble is that I cannot yet see any difference between the "straw" argument and the original argument of Block and Fodor's that I methodologically dismissed.

Since this book went to press, I have learned of a new sort of objection to my application of the Kripkean "a posteriori necessity" picture to qualia. The objection is based on the two-dimensional modal logic adumbrated by Davies and Humberstone (1980). Preliminary versions of it have already appeared in White

1986, and in Lewis 1994. I am told that there is a fuller version in Jackson 1993. The most explicit version I have seen is given by Chalmers, in press. I do not accept the objection, because I believe Davies and Humberstone's modal notions are confused, but to say why will require a separate paper.

21

On such similarity relations, see Stalnaker 1968, Lewis 1973, and for further interpretation, see Lycan 1984, 1993.

22

I will take this opportunity, for the record, to correct a misunderstanding on Kobes's part, though it matters not a bit to his present argument. (I also hasten to note that this misinterpretation has been made by at least one other reviewer of *Consciousness* as well, so it must have been somehow encouraged by the text.)

Kobes characterizes me as *defending* adverbialism. As I have said, I have always been concerned to attack adverbialism, not to endorse it. I viewed adverbialism as a sham, an evasion of the phenomenal-individual problem—a sham because even if one casts all the visual-field description as a long complex adverbial modifier, the adverbial still has plenty of bound variables, occurring more than orthographically within it, that refer to phenomenal individuals, so its adverbialness simply does not help and is pointless.

However, I now see that Kobes's reading has some conceptual foundation even if it lacks textual support: If I continue to appeal to Australian paraphrases as cashed by me in terms of possible worlds, this is *deep-syntactically* a form of adverbialism, although not one that eliminates ostensible reference to phenomenal individuals, as Chisholm intended.

23

For the record my replies are as follows: (1) The stipulation that no retinal stimulation can cause newhue sensations does not entail that newhue objects are nomologically impossible; the latter depends on one's metaphysical analysis of color, and no extant metaphysical analysis of color, even my Armstrongian one, is very satisfactory.

(2) Even if newhue objects are indeed nomologically impossible, the then counternomological conditional "Leopold is sensing as if a newhue object were present" might still be true; this depends on one's theory of counterfactuals. An epistemic theory of counterfactuals (such as my own [Lycan 1984]) might have no trouble with it, especially if there is a logically coherent concept of what nomologically impossible retinal stimulation would produce newhue sensations.

(3) If newhue objects are nomologically impossible, then cortically induced newhue sensations do not yield or reflect any actual

discriminative capacity. Therefore, they correspond to no functional human ability. Though they are not an abnormality in the sense suggested above (because they constitute a superfluity rather than a lack, and the people that have them are normal subjects), they confer no discriminative benefit either and they are not experienced under normal *conditions,* being the result of brain tampering rather than sensory input. Thus we might patch my analysis by adding "as if he were normal and were *by a biologically normal perceptual process* sensing a physical green object before him."

24

As Kobes pointed out in a discussion of his paper "Are There Homogeneously Green Phenomenal Individuals?" delivered at the 1991 meeting of the American Philosophical Association, Pacific Division. He also noted that the rigidifying move does badly by the original "newhue" example, for a cortically stimulated human being might be experiencing newhue but would not be sensing as we normal human beings would be sensing if confronted by a newhue physical object. (To reply to this, I would have to rely on points made in the previous note.)

25

Incidentally, Crimmins's article is by far the best I know to have appeared on the ugly topic of tacit belief, since 1986.

CHAPTER FIVE

1

For these technicalities see Boër and Lycan 1986.

2

For some relevant syntactic work, see Karttunen 1977, Hirschbühler 1979, and Groenendijk and Stokhof 1982.

3

Levin goes on to distinguish a strong from a weak sense of "direct," but this distinction does not matter to the present point, vital though it is to her main argument against Nagel and Jackson.

4

Conee (1985, 298) adds that in some abnormal cases the abilities might be explained otherwise. For example, without knowing what it is like to see red or blue, Mary might surgically be given the *ability* to visualize these colors even though she never goes on to exercise this ability. Nor do the various abilities seem necessary for "knowing what it's like": Mary might know what the blue of sky looks like while she is seeing the sky but, through neurological deficit, be deprived of any ability to visualize, compare, or the like. See also Conee 1994, 138–139.

5

Nemirow (1990, 493) says that the ability hypothesis affords a "more elegant" explanation of the ineffability than does bare reference to "the inexpressible qualities of experience." I vigorously agree that it does; what I dispute is that it gives a more elegant explanation than does Russell's explanation or a functionalist one or any of a number of other possible substantive explanations. I have given my own explanation in chapter 3.

6

I almost used a different example, the taste of Vegemite, for I have a Vegemite comparison that is both vivid and deadly accurate, but if I had expounded it and David Lewis were to read this paper, he would lose his vaunted innocence, and it would be all my fault.

7

Though it starts from the same premise, this argument differs from the "second objection" that Nemirow (1990, 497) anticipates.

8

For defense of an interesting related thesis, see Nida-Rümelin (in press).

9

The "explanatory gap" discussed in chapter 3 is another question.

10

However, see the excellent discussion in Robinson 1993.

CHAPTER SIX

1

See also Peacocke 1983, chaps. 1 and 2, to be discussed in section 3 below. Peacocke uses the terms "representational" and "sensational." McGinn (1982, 44) made a similar suggestion on similar grounds. The general idea goes back at least to Chisholm's (1957) distinction between "comparative" and "noncomparative" senses of "looks."

2

Its most noticeable standing ambiguity has been between its strict use, meaning a first-order qualitative property of a phenomenal individual such as a sense datum, and a more general use, meaning whatever it is about experience that constitutes phenomenal character in any sense.

3

My argument elaborates one given briefly by Block (1990, 55).

4

Block claims to avoid the question of the inverted spectrum's metaphysical possibility— successfully, since he does not invert anyone's internal spectrum. But this does nothing to show that his own example is metaphysically possible.

5
Since intentional content is "wide," i.e., does not supervene on the molecular constitution of a subject's nervous system, intentional contents could themselves invert with respect to the subject's narrow functional states, as in a Twin Earth example.

6
Here again, the New Strange theory mentioned in section 1 may evade the objection, for it may be more obvious that "Strange Qualia" in the new, second sense of Shoemaker and Block are narrow, we will see.

7
Harman writes, "When Eloise sees a tree before her, the colors she experiences are all experienced as features of the tree and its surroundings. None of them are experienced as intrinsic features of her experience. And that is true of you too. . . . Look at a tree and try to turn your attention to intrinsic features of your visual experience. I predict you will find that the only features there to turn your attention to will be features of the presented tree, including relational features of the tree 'from here'" (1990, 39).

8
I do not think it is fanciful. As Robert Van Gulick has observed in correspondence, there may be excellent reason to regard an individual neuron as computing quite complex properties of the pattern of activity in its dendritic arbor.

9
Block 1990, in correspondence, and in his comments on a version of this material presented at the American Philosophical Association Eastern Division meetings, 1993.

10
A second way of understanding Block's idea has been suggested to me by Bosuk Yoon: Think of a New Strange Quale as a mode of presentation, conceived psychologically instead of (as Frege intended) as an abstract entity. We all know that one and the same intentional object can be represented under different guises or modes of presentation, as when I say "here," meaning where I am standing, and you say "over there," meaning the very same spot. So why cannot one color, as intentional object, be represented by you under mode of presentation q_1 but by me under mode of presentation q_2? And is that not a good model for New Strange Qualia inverted with respect to phenomenal color, since, according to me, phenomenal color is just a representatum or intentional object? (I myself have made much of the pronoun analogy in chapters 3 and 5 above, and see also section 8 below.)

11

Since Block disavows both the original Strange Qualia and the New Strange theory, one may well wonder what it is he does hold. I should mention that over the years Block and I have experienced severe mutual difficulty in understanding each other's main claims about the ontological structure of experience. Much of that difficulty has been terminological, but it is also clear that we look at the topic in different ways—surprisingly different, given the similarity of our interests, backgrounds, and philosophical upbringing.

Here is my current understanding, based on recent correspondence. (In light of the sad track record I have just mentioned, I make no claim for it save that it is my current understanding.)

The "looks" locution, as in "The tomato looks red," is intentional/representational, Block agrees. But it cannot be used to describe kaleidoscopic spectrum inversion, because, as we saw in section 1 of this chapter, under kaleidoscopic inversion, the normal association between putative color looks and objective physical colors would break down, there being no basis for thinking that any one percipient gets an object's color right to the exclusion of the other subjects. So there would be no "normal" associations between "looks" and objective colors either. Given the psychosemantic hypothesis that to "look red" is to be represented as red objects are normally visually represented, that means that what gets kaleidoscopically inverted cannot be "looks" in the sense of representational contents. So what gets inverted must be "looks" in a more rarefied sense that outruns (all) representational contents. That shows that even the normal veridical visual experience of a ripe tomato includes such an element that can or might invert with respect to the tomato's looking red and so outstrips it (and is inexpressible in English). A Strange Quale is not a quale in the C. I. Lewis's sense (see chapter 4), because it is not a first-order property of an apparent phenomenal individual; it is a property of the experiencing as a whole, so it is at best a higher-order property of the apparent phenomenal individual.

However, Block does have an oblique way of applying "looks" to these higher-order Strange Qualia, in terms of a similarity relation in the manner of Shoemaker 1975. Though "looks red" is intentional, "looks *the same*" can be either intentional/representational or Strange-Qualitative, as in "Red things look the same to you as green things look to me."

Block agrees that it is weird to suggest that my green images might look red to you. And he agrees that it sounds weird to suggest that what experience you have in hosting, say, a red afterimage is the same as the experience I have in hosting a green one. But that, he says, is because of a systematic ambiguity in "same" and expressions containing it. In particular, "looks the same" can express either intentional-content identity or Strange-Qualitative identity. His idea is only that what visually represents red in one person might be phenomenally the same as what visually represents green in another—in a special sense of "phenomenal" that is more rarified than mine. (For me, remember, the represented redness *is* the phenomenal character of the experience in the only sense of "phenomenal" I wish to allow; so I take phenomenal-identity conditions simply to be representational- or intentional-identity conditions. But for Block, there are nonintentional-qualitative-identity conditions that crisscross the intentional-identity conditions.)

The view just sketched does sound less weird than the New Strange theory, but I am not sure whether it is much less weird. The red of an afterimage or of a hallucinated tomato can be exactly the same shade and saturation as that of a real tomato, and would be described in just the same terms by a phenomenologist. Yet it is a mental, in my usage phenomenal, redness, and when philosophers talk of such properties, they think they are engaged in phenomenal talk, since they are talking about the qualitative character of visual experience, as opposed to the objective color of an external object. Block now maintains that the term "phenomenal" is systematically ambiguous as between that usage and his more rarefied one. So there is still supposed to be a sense in which my afterimage or hallucination might look to me the way green afterimages look to him, even though in my sense it is phenomenally red. I think I will leave this issue for now, except to add the following speculative diagnosis. Block tells me that it is *not* true of him, but it does fit several other philosophers who in conversation have declared themselves sympathetic to Block's line as they understand it.

Some people think of mere *representation* as a fairly cheap and shallow affair. For representation is ubiquitous and easily achieved. I can write "red" in chalk on the blackboard, or point to a pot of rouge, or Morse-code R-E-D to a neighboring ship, or represent the property redness in any of a thousand other simple ways. So is W.G.L. saying that *all it is* for me to have a bright red patch in my visual field is for me to represent the property redness? But that is *obviously* insufficient. On this view, representation in and of itself is utterly bloodless, hardly the sort of thing of which *qualia* are made; it could not be representation alone and per se that gives an afterimage its qualitative character, its subjective color. Surely the real *color look* of the afterimage could invert with respect to mere representational "of-red-ness, the latter being merely what the intentional object happens to be mentally *called*. So even if no English word such as "red" can be used to express that look, it is obvious that the look transcends the mere representing and is the real qualitative character of the afterimage.

NOTE TO PAGE 125

If that were what Block was thinking, I would reply that unlike linguistic representation, perceptual representation is neither cheap nor shallow but very complicated—a difficult achievement possible only for creatures with perceptual systems very like our own (see again Gilman 1994). *Under our distinctive visual mode of presentation,* of-red-ness is, I have argued, an excellent candidate for what philosophers normally call the redness of the afterimage, the image's introspectible color.

12

To my knowledge, that assumption had never been dragged out into the light and examined before this book went to press, save briefly by Teller (1984), but in the course of discussion at the Eighth SOFIA Conference (Cancún, Mexico, June 1995), no fewer than six arguments were produced in its favor, most prominently the one that flows from Stalnaker's new support of Block. That was real philosophical progress, of a sort almost never achieved at a single conference. Viva SOFIA!—except that I must now eventually confront and vanquish all the remaining arguments.

Block (1994) offers a version of the Inverted Earth argument that does not appeal to the supervenience assumption and is more like Stalnaker's interpretation.

13

One suggestion would be to understand the semantic shift in terms of Hartry Field's (1973) notion of "partial reference." I do not find that notion at all plausible, but there is not space to digress on this matter here.

14

Block adds, "So if my story is right, Lycan (if he is to be an externalist about memory) should say that the subject's color experience has shifted gradually without the subject's knowing about it" (in press). This is an odd remark, since I already had said that the subject's color experience has shifted; that was my original response to the Inverted Earth example. Externalism about memory has come up only since, in light of Block's present criticism of my position.

15

Block adds a parting shot against those whose psychosemantics require that the Inverted Earth subject's representational contents would never switch, no matter how long he or she stayed on Inverted Earth. Though I do not take the latter position myself, the argument is worth mentioning. It is roughly that a representationally *unswitched* subject would have an inverted spectrum relative to the Inverted Earth aboriginals, even though "you are as functionally similar to them as you like." But if spectrum inversion is achieved so easily, we could accomplish the same without leaving Earth: just raise twins, one with inverting lenses. The twins would "end up functionally and representationally identical, but phenomenally different."

Just three quick remarks against that argument: First, remember the double relativity of the notion of an "inverted spectrum." Block's example is so far underdescribed in this regard. It sounds as though he means that on Inverted Earth the sky would look blue to the subject (because of the inverting lenses) and the subject would continue to represent blue but learn to *say* "yellow" with the natives, while on Earth the inverted twin would experience yellow because of the lenses but learn to *say* "blue" with the normals. But presumably the inverted twin on Earth would be representing yellow as well. So on this possibly mistaken construal, I do not see a Block-style gap between representational and qualitative content in the twin. (Perhaps he has in mind that the inverted twin would be representing blue rather than yellow, so that the qualitative experienced yellow would diverge from it. But that claim would require psychosemantic defense; it does not follow from the present conservative psychosemantic hypothesis alone.) Second, whether two twins just one of whom has inverting lenses are "functionally identical" depends on where the lenses are placed, on how they work, and on one's chosen notion of "function" as well. Third, whether the twins are representationally identical depends on details of one's psychosemantics even if that psychosemantics is stipulated to be of the conservative Millikanian sort, though I would not want to rest much weight on this third point.

16
Block (1995a, 281) offers a quick further antirepresentationist argument about pains: He says that there are pains that differ phenomenally but "not in any way describable in words." I am not so pessimistic. Some people are very good at describing their pains, describing them paradigmatically in representational terms like "throbbing," "burning," "sharp," "dull," "stinging," and the like. It would be even easier to describe the difference between two pains, since a comparison is afforded. No doubt our descriptive powers would run out before long, but the two pains would still feel as though different unfortunate things were happening in the respective parts of the body.

17
Bernard Kobes (1991) has made a related objection that has considerable merit, but it is science-fictional and succeeds only by being so.

18
For a similar and well worked-out view, see Rey 1992b.

1

Michael Tye (1992, 173) has made one doughty response, but I do not find it entirely convincing.

2

See chapter 3 of Perkins 1983.

3

The other is lengthy and is given in Lycan 1989.

4

I am not entirely sure of that last claim. One can grant that a *detector* or indicator is registering a false positive without being forced to admit full-blown representation, if one wishes to place further conditions on what it takes for something to be a genuine representation. My claim for this first argument is only that smell has a possibly inexistent intentional object in at least the rudimentary sense that detectors and indicators have intentional objects. (However, I would add that the strong and multifarious functional connections of smell to memory and other cognitive agencies suggest a representational connection as well.)

5

See Ittelson 1968. The present illustration and description are taken from Gombrich 1960.

6

For a related example, see Dorothy L. Sayers, "The Haunted Policeman," reprinted in *Lord Peter* (New York: Avon Books, 1972).

7

In more recent work, Peacocke (1992) has put forward some ideas that seem hospitable to the layering thesis, though they do not include it. (1) He posits a nonconceptual kind of representational content, embodied in his notion of a "spatial type" or "scenario." (2) He posits a second and more primitive kind of nonconceptual representational content in the form of "protopropositions," incorporating concepts such as "square," "curved," and "parallel to," though those terms apply to ostensible everyday objects and their surfaces, rather than to what I am calling "shapes."

8

Jackson (1977) got this right, even though he believed the shapes to be actual phenomenal individuals, sense data.

As has been widely pointed out, vision presents us with very-fine-grained content that outruns our own ability to express it in words. I do not suppose that all the shapes and expanses we see fall under our own everyday concepts.

9

It is sometimes objected against the intentional-inexistent view of sense data that apparent colors inhere in things that are obviously not physical objects. For example, we say that *the sky* is blue, but no one thinks that there is any nonexistent *physical thing* up there. But I contend that there is a nonexistent physical thing up there: It is an illusion. Vision represents "the sky" as an object. Poets write about it. Visually, the sky is *a canopy,* or the *vault* of heaven.

10

Thus my view differs from that of Austin (1962). Austin emphasizes that in response to the question "What do you see?" the answers "(1) 'A bright speck'; (2) 'A star'; (3) 'Sirius'; (4) 'The image in the fourteenth mirror of the telescope'... all... may be perfectly correct" (1962, 99), but this is because he considers the speck, the star, Sirius, and the image all to be one and the same individual.

References

Adams, E. M. (1975). *Philosophy and the Modern Mind*. Chapel Hill, N.C.: University of North Carolina Press.

Adams, E. M. (1991). *The Metaphysics of Self and World*. Philadelphia: Temple University Press.

Anscombe, G. E. M. (1965). "The Intentionality of Sensation: A Grammatical Feature." In R. J. Butler (ed.), *Analytical Philosophy: Second Series*. Oxford: Basil Blackwell.

Armstrong, D. M. (1961). *Perception and the Physical World*. London: Routledge and Kegan Paul.

Armstrong, D. M. (1962). *Bodily Sensations*. London: Routledge and Kegan Paul.

Armstrong, D. M. (1968a). "The Headless Woman Illusion and the Defense of Materialism." *Analysis* 29:48–49.

Armstrong, D. M. (1968b). *A Materialist Theory of the Mind*. London: Routledge and Kegan Paul.

Armstrong, D. M. (1978). *Universals and Scientific Realism.*, 2 vols. Cambridge: Cambridge University Press.

Armstrong, D. M. (1980). "What Is Consciousness?" In D. M. Armstrong, *The Nature of Mind and Other Essays*. Ithaca, N.Y.: Cornell University Press.

Armstrong, D. M. (1987). "Smart and the Secondary Qualities." In P. Pettit, R. Sylvan, and J. Norman (eds.), *Metaphysics and Morality: Essays in Honour of J. J. C. Smart*. Oxford: Basil Blackwell.

Armstrong, D. M., and N. Malcolm (1984). *Consciousness and Causality*. Oxford: Basil Blackwell.

Austin, J. L. (1962). *Sense and Sensibilia*. Oxford: Oxford University Press.

Baars, B. J. (1983). "Conscious Contents Provide the Nervous System with Coherent, Global Information." In Davidson, Schwartz and Shapiro 1983.

Baars, B. J. (1988). *A Cognitive Theory of Consciousness*. Cambridge: Cambridge University Press.

Baars, B. J., and M. Fehling (1992). "Consciousness Is Associated with Central as well as Distributed Processes." *Behavioral and Brain Sciences* 15:203–204.

Block, N. (1978). "Troubles with Functionalism." In W. Savage (ed.), *Perception and Cognition*, Minnesota Studies in the Philosophy of Science, no. 9. Minneapolis: University of Minnesota Press.

Block, N. (1990). "Inverted Earth." In Tomberlin 1990.

Block, N. (1993). Review of Dennett's *Consciousness Explained*. *Journal of Philosophy* 90:181–193.

Block, N. (1994). "Qualia." In Guttenplan 1994.

Block, N. (1995a). "How Many Concepts of Consciousness?" *Behavioral and Brain Sciences* 18:272–284.

Block, N. (1995b) "On a Confusion about a Function of Consciousness." *Behavioral and Brain Sciences* 18:227–247.

Block, N. (in press). "Mental Paint and Mental Latex." In Villanueva, in press.

Block, N., O. Flanagan, and G. Güzeldere (eds.) (1996). *The Nature of Consciousness*. Cambridge: MIT Press.

Block, N., and J. A. Fodor (1972). "What Psychological States Are Not." *Philosophical Review* 81:159–181.

Boër, S., and W. G. Lycan (1980). "Who, Me?" *Philosophical Review* 89:427–466.

Boër, S., and W. G. Lycan (1986). *Knowing Who*. Cambridge: MIT Press.

Boër, S., and W. G. Lycan (1987). "Yes, Who? (Reply to Yagisawa)." *Philosophia* 17:187–190.

Broad, C. D. (1925). *The Mind and Its Place in Nature*. London: Routledge and Kegan Paul.

Broadbent, D. E. (1958). *Perception and Communication*. Oxford: Pergamon Press.

Broadbent, D. E. (1982). "Task Combination and Selective Intake of Information." *Acta Psychologica* 50:253–290.

Burge, T. (1979). "Individualism and the Mental." In P. French, T. E. Uehling, and H. Wettstein (eds.), *Studies in Metaphysics*, Midwest Studies in Philosophy, no. 4. Minneapolis: University of Minnesota Press.

Butchvarov, P. (1980), "Adverbial Theories of Consciousness." In P. A. French, T. E. Uehling, and H. Wettstein (eds.), *Studies in Epistemology,* Midwest Studies in Philosophy, no. 5. Minneapolis: University of Minnesota Press.

Campbell, K. K. (1969). "Colours." In R. Brown and C. D. Rollins (eds.), *Contemporary Philosophy in Australia.* New York: Humanities Press.

Castañeda, H.-N. (1966). "'He': A Study in the Logic of Self-Consciousness." *Ratio* 8:130–157.

Chalmers, D. (in press). *Toward a Theory of Consciousness.* Oxford: Oxford University Press.

Chisholm, R. M. (1957). *Perceiving.* Ithaca: Cornell University Press.

Churchland, P. M. (1985). "Reduction, Qualia, and the Direct Introspection of Brain States." *Journal of Philosophy* 82:8–28.

Conee, E. (1985). "Physicalism and Phenomenal Qualities." *Philosophical Quarterly* 35:296–302.

Conee, E. (1994). "Phenomenal Knowledge." *Australasian Journal of Philosophy* 72:136–150.

Crane, T. (ed.) (1992). *The Contents of Experience.* (Cambridge: Cambridge University Press).

Crick, F., and C. Koch (1990). "Towards a Neurobiological Theory of Consciousness." *Seminars in the Neurosciences* 2:263–275.

Crimmins, M. (1992). "Tacitness and Virtual Beliefs." *Mind and Language* 7:240–263.

Davidson, R., G. E. Schwartz, and D. Shapiro (eds.) (1983). *Consciousness and Self-Regulation.* Vol. 3. New York: Plenum Press.

Davies, M., and I. L. Humberstone (1980). "Two Notions of Necessity." *Philosophical Studies* 38:1–30.

Davies, M., and G. Humphreys (eds.) (1992). *Consciousness.* Oxford: Basil Blackwell.

Dennett, D. C. (1978a). *Brainstorms.* Montgomery, Vt.: Bradford Books.

Dennett, D. C. (1978b). "Where Am I?" In Dennett 1978a. Reprinted in Hofstadter and Dennett 1981.

Dennett, D. C. (1991). *Consciousness Explained.* Boston: Little, Brown, and Co.

Dennett, D. C. (1993). Review of Searle's *Rediscovery of the Mind*. *Journal of Philosophy* 90:193–205.

Dennett, D. C., and M. Kinsbourne (1992a). "Time and the Observer: The Where and When of Consciousness in the Brain." *Behavioral and Brain Sciences* 15:183–201.

Dennett, D. C., and M. Kinsbourne (1992b). "Authors' Response." *Behavioral and Brain Sciences* 15:234–243.

Dretske, F. (1988). *Explaining Behavior*. Cambridge: MIT Press.

Dretske, F. (1993). "Conscious Experience." *Mind* 102:263–283.

Dretske, F. (in press). "Phenomenal Externalism." In Villanueva, in press.

Farrell, B. A. (1950). "Experience." *Mind* 59:170–198. Reprinted in V. C. Chappell (ed.), *The Philosophy of Mind* (Englewood Cliffs, N.J.: Prentice-Hall, 1962).

Field, H. (1973). "Theory Change and the Indeterminacy of Reference." *Journal of Philosophy* 70:462–481.

Flanagan, O. (1992). *Consciousness Reconsidered*. Cambridge: MIT Press.

Fodor, J. A. (1980). "Methodological Solipsism Considered as a Research Strategy in Cognitive Psychology." *Behavioral and Brain Sciences* 3:63–73.

Fodor, J. A. (1983). *The Modularity of Mind*. Cambridge: MIT Press.

Geach, P. (1957). "On Belief about Oneself." *Analysis* 18:23–24.

Geldard, F. A., and C. E. Sherrick (1972). "The Cutaneous 'Rabbit': A Perceptual Illusion." *Science* 178:178–179.

Gert, B. (1965). "Imagination and Verifiability." *Philosophical Studies* 16:44–47.

Gilman D. (1994). "Pictures in Cognition." *Erkenntnis* 41:87–102.

Gilman, D. (in press). "Consciousness and Mental Representation." *Behavioral and Brain Sciences*.

Goldman, A. I. (1993). "Consciousness, Folk Psychology, and Cognitive Science." *Consciousness and Cognition* 2:364–382.

Gombrich, E. H. (1960). *Art and Illusion*. Princeton: Princeton University Press.

Gregory, R. L. (1986). *Odd Perceptions*. London: Methuen.

Groenendijk, J., and M. Stokhof (1982). "Semantic Analysis of *Wh*- Complements." *Linguistics and Philosophy* 5:175–234.

Gunderson, K. (1970). "Asymmetries and Mind-Body Perplexities." In M. Radner and S. Winokur (eds.), *Analyses of Theories and Methods of Physics and Psychology*, Minnesota Studies in the Philosophy of Science, no. 4. Minneapolis: University of Minnesota Press.

Guttenplan, S. (ed.) (1994). *A Companion to the Philosophy of Mind*. Oxford: Basil Blackwell.

Hardin, C. L. (1988). *Color for Philosophers*. Indianapolis: Hackett Publishing.

Harman, G. (1990). "The Intrinsic Quality of Experience." In Tomberlin 1990.

Harrison, B. (1973). *Form and Content*. Oxford: Basil Blackwell.

Hart, W. D. (1988). *Engines of the Soul*. Cambridge: Cambridge University Press.

Hilbert, D. R. (1987). *Color and Color Perception*. Stanford: Center for the Study of Language and Information.

Hill, C. S. (1987). "Introspective Awareness of Sensations." *Topoi* 6:9–22.

Hill, C. S. (1991). *Sensations*. Cambridge: Cambridge University Press.

Hintikka, K. J. J. (1969). "On the Logic of Perception." In N. S. Care and R. H. Grimm (eds.), *Perception and Personal Identity*. Cleveland: Case Western Reserve University Press.

Hintikka, K. J. J. (1975). *The Intentions of Intentionality and Other New Models for Modalities*. Dordrecht: D. Reidel.

Hirschbühler, P. (1979). *The Syntax and Semantics of Wh- Constructions*. Bloomington: Indiana University Linguistics Club Publications.

Hofstadter, D. R., and D. C. Dennett (eds.) (1981). *The Mind's I: Fantasies and Reflections on Self and Soul*. New York: Basic Books.

Horgan, T. (1984). "Jackson on Physical Information and Qualia." *Philosophical Quarterly* 34:147–183.

Horgan, T. (1987). "Supervenient Qualia." *Philosophical Review* 96:491–520.

Ittelson, W. H. (1968). *The Ames Demonstrations in Perception*. Princeton and London: Hafner Publishing.

Jackson, F. (1977). *Perception*. Cambridge: Cambridge University Press.

Jackson, F. (1982). "Epiphenomenal Qualia." *Philosophical Quarterly* 32:127–136. Reprinted in Lycan 1990.

Jackson, F. (1993). "Armchair Metaphysics." In J. O'Leary-Hawthorne and M. Michael (eds.), *Philosophy in Mind*. Dordrecht: Kluwer.

Jackson, F., and R. Pargetter (1987). "An Objectivist's Guide to Subjectivism about Colour." *Revue Internationale de Philosophie* 41:127–141.

John, E. R. (1976). "A Model of Consciousness." In G. E. Schwartz and D. Shapiro (eds.), *Consciousness and Self-Regulation,* vol. 1. New York: Plenum Press.

Johnson, M. (1987). *The Body in the Mind.* Chicago: University of Chicago Press.

Johnston, W. A., and V. J. Dark (1986). "Selective Attention." *Annual Review of Psychology* 37:43–75.

Kant, I. (1965). *Critique of Pure Reason,* Trans. Norman Kemp Smith. New York: St. Martin's Press. First published in 1781.

Karttunen, L. (1977). "Syntax and Semantics of Questions." *Linguistics and Philosophy* 1:3–44.

Kirk, R. (1994). *Raw Feeling.* Oxford: Clarendon Press.

Knapp, P. H. (1976). "The Mysterious 'Split': A Clinical Inquiry into Problems of Consciousness and Brain." In G. Globus, G. Maxwell, and I. Savodnik (eds.), *Consciousness and the Brain.* New York: Plenum Press.

Kobes, B. (1991). "Sensory Qualities and 'Homunctionalism': A Review Essay of W. G. Lycan's *Consciousness.*" *Philosophical Psychology* 4:147–158.

Kolers, P., and M. von Grünau (1976). "Shape and Color in Apparent Motion." *Vision Research* 16:329–335.

Kraut, R. (1982). "Sensory States and Sensory Objects." *Noûs* 16:277–295.

Kripke, S. (1972). "Naming and Necessity." In D. Davidson and G. Harman (eds.), *Semantics of Natural Language.* Dordrecht: D. Reidel.

Lackner, J. R., and M. Garrett (1973). "Resolving Ambiguity: Effects of Biasing Context in the Unattended Ear." *Cognition* 1:359–372.

Leeds, S. (1993). "Qualia, Awareness, Sellars." *Noûs* 27:303–330.

Levin, J. (1986). "Could Love Be like a Heatwave? Physicalism and the Subjective Character of Experience." *Philosophical Studies* 49:245–261. Reprinted in Lycan 1990.

Levine, J. (1983). "Materialism and Qualia: The Explanatory Gap." *Pacific Philosophical Quarterly* 64:354–361.

Lewis, C. I. (1929). *Mind and the World Order.* New York: C. Scribner's Sons.

Lewis, D. (1973). *Counterfactuals.* Cambridge: Harvard University Press.

Lewis, D. (1983a). "Individuation by Acquaintance and by Stipulation." *Philosophical Review* 92:3–32.

Lewis, D. (1983b). "Postscript to 'Mad Pain and Martian Pain'." In D. Lewis, *Philosophical Papers,* vol. 1. Oxford: Oxford University Press.

Lewis, D. (1990). "What Experience Teaches." In Lycan 1990.

Lewis, D. (1994). "Lewis, David: Reduction of Mind." In Guttenplan 1994.

Libet, B. (1965). "Cortical Activation in Conscious and Unconscious Experience." *Perspectives in Biology and Medicine* 9:77–86.

Libet, B. (1985). "Unconscious Cerebral Initiative and the Role of Conscious Will in Voluntary Action." *Behavioral and Brain Sciences* 10:529–566.

Libet, B. (1992). "Models of Conscious Timing and the Experimental Evidence." *Behavioral and Brain Sciences* 15:213–215.

Loar, B. (1990). "Phenomenal States." In Tomberlin 1990.

Locke, J. (1959). *An Essay concerning Human Understanding.* Ed. A. C. Fraser. New York: Dover Publications. First published in 1689.

Lycan, W. G. (1971), "Gombrich, Wittgenstein, and the Duck-Rabbit." *Journal of Aesthetics and Art Criticism* 30:229–237. Reprinted in J. V. Canfield (ed.), *The Philosophy of Wittgenstein: Aesthetics, Ethics, and Religion* (New York: Garland Publishing, 1985).

Lycan, W. G. (1973). "Inverted Spectrum." *Ratio* 15:315–319.

Lycan, W. G. (1981). "Toward a Homuncular Theory of Believing." *Cognition and Brain Theory* 4:139–159.

Lycan, W. G. (1984). "A Syntactically Motivated Theory of Conditionals." In P. A. French, T. E. Uehling, and H. Wettstein (eds.), *Causation and Causal Theories,* Midwest Studies in Philosophy, no. 9. Minneapolis: University of Minnesota Press.

Lycan, W. G. (1985a). "Abortion and the Civil Rights of Machines." In N. Potter and M. Timmons (eds.), *Morality and Universality*. Dordrecht: D. Reidel.

Lycan, W. G. (1985b). "The Paradox of Naming." In B.-K. Matilal and J. L. Shaw (eds.), *Analytical Philosophy in Comparative Perspective*. Dordrecht: D. Reidel.

Lycan, W. G. (1987). *Consciousness*. Cambridge: MIT Press.

Lycan, W. G. (1988). *Judgment and Justification*. Cambridge: Cambridge University Press.

Lycan, W. G. (1989). "Philosophy and Smell." Unpublished monograph, excerpts from which constituted the Presidential Address delivered at the Fifteenth Annual Meeting of the Society for Philosophy and Psychology, Tucson, Arizona, April 1989.

Lycan, W. G. (ed.) (1990). *Mind and Cognition*. Oxford: Basil Blackwell.

Lycan, W. G. (1993). "MPP, RIP." In J. Tomberlin (ed.), *Language and Logic,* Philosophical Perspectives, no. 7. Atascadero: Ridgeview Publishing.

Lycan, W. G. (1994). *Modality and Meaning*. Dordrecht: Kluwer Publishing.

Lycan, W. G. (in preparation, a). "Sense-Data: Pro, Con, and Beyond."

Lycan, W. G. (in preparation, b). "True Colors."

Marks, C. (1979). *Commissurotomy, Consciousness, and the Unity of Mind*. Montgomery, Vt.: Bradford Books.

Marras, A. (1993). "Materialism, Functionalism, and Supervenient Qualia." *Dialogue* 32:475–492.

McClamrock, R. (1995). *Existential Cognition*. Chicago: University of Chicago Press.

McGinn, C. (1982). *The Character of Mind*. Oxford: Oxford University Press.

McGinn, C. (1983). *The Subjective View*. Oxford: Oxford University Press.

McGinn, C. (1989). "Can We Solve the Mind-Body Problem?" *Mind* 98:349–366. Reprinted in McGinn, *The Problem of Consciousness* (Oxford: Basil Blackwell, 1991).

McMullen, C. (1985). "'Knowing What It's Like' and the Essential Indexical." *Philosophical Studies* 48:211–234.

Millikan, R. G. (1984). *Language, Thought, and Other Biological Categories.* Cambridge: MIT Press.

Millikan, R. G. (1989). "Biosemantics." *Journal of Philosophy* 86:281–297.

Nagel, T. (1965). "Physicalism." *Philosophical Review* 74:339–356.

Nagel, T. (1974). "What Is It Like to Be a Bat?" *Philosophical Review* 82:435–456.

Nagel, T. (1979). "Panpsychism." In T. Nagel, *Mortal Questions.* Cambridge: Cambridge University Press.

Neisser, U. (1967). *Cognitive Psychology.* New York: Appleton Century Crofts.

Nelkin, N. (1989). "Unconscious Sensations." *Philosophical Psychology* 2:129–141.

Nemirow, L. (1980). Review of Nagel's *Mortal Questions. Philosophical Review* 89:473–477.

Nemirow, L. (1990). "Physicalism and the Cognitive Role of Acquaintance." In Lycan 1990.

Nida-Rümelin, M. (in press). "Is the Naturalization of Qualitative Experience Possible or Sensible?" In the proceedings of the Third Pittsburgh-Konstanz Conference in the Philosophy of Science, tentatively entitled *Philosophy and the Sciences of the Mind,* ed. M. Carrier and P. Machamer. Pittsburgh: University of Pittsburgh Press.

Palmer, D. (1975). "Unfelt Pains." *American Philosophical Quarterly* 12:289–298.

Parasuraman, R., and D. R. Davies (1984). *Varieties of Attention.* New York: Academic Press.

Peacocke, C. (1983). *Sense and Content.* Oxford: Oxford University Press.

Peacocke, C. (1992). "Scenarios, Concepts, and Perception." In Crane 1992.

Peirce, C. S. (1931). "Objective Logic." In C. S. Pierce, *Collected Papers,* vol. 6, *Scientific Metaphysics,* ed. C. Hartshorne and P. Weiss. Cambridge: Harvard University Press. First published in 1898.

Pereboom, D. (1994). "Bats, Brain Scientists, and the Limitations of Introspection." *Philosophy and Phenomenological Research* 54:315–329.

Perkins, M. (1983). *Sensing the World*. Indianapolis: Hackett Publishing.

Perry, J. (1979). "The Problem of the Essential Indexical." *Noûs* 13:3–21.

Pitcher, G. (1970). "Pain Perception." *Philosophical Review* 79: 368–393.

Pitcher, G. (1971). *A Theory of Perception*. Princeton: Princeton University Press.

Place, U. T. (1956). "Is Consciousness a Brain Process?" *British Journal of Psychology* 47:44–50.

Putnam, H. (1960). "Minds and Machines." In S. Hook (ed.), *Dimensions of Mind*. Collier Books.

Putnam, H. (1965). "Brains and Behavior." In R. J. Butler (ed.), *Analytical Philosophy: Second Series*. Oxford: Basil Blackwell.

Putnam, H. (1975). "The Meaning of 'Meaning'." In K. Gunderson (ed.), *Language, Mind, and Knowledge,* Minnesota Studies in the Philosophy of Science, no. 7. Minneapolis: University of Minnesota Press.

Rey, G. (1983). "A Reason for Doubting the Existence of Consciousness." In Davidson, Schwartz, and Shapiro 1983.

Rey, G. (1988). "A Question about Consciousness." In H. R. Otto and J. A. Tuedio (eds.), *Perspectives on Mind*. Dordrecht: D. Reidel.

Rey, G. (1991). "Sensations in a Language of Thought." In Villaneuva 1991.

Rey, G. (1992a). "Sensational Sentences." In Davies and Humphreys 1992.

Rey, G. (1992b). "Sensational Sentences Switched." *Philosophical Studies* 68:289–319.

Rey, G. (1994). "Dennett's Unrealistic Psychology." *Philosophical Topics* 22:259–289.

Richardson, R. (1981). "Internal Representation: Prologue to a Theory of Intentionality." *Philosophical Topics* 12:171–211.

Robinson, D. (1993). "Epiphenomenalism, Laws, and Properties." *Philosophical Studies* 69:1–34.

Rock, I. (1983). *The Logic of Perception*. Cambridge: MIT Press.

Rollins, M. (1989). *Mental Imagery*. New Haven: Yale University Press.

Rorty, R. (1970). "Incorrigibility as the Mark of the Mental." *Journal of Philosophy* 67:399–424.

Rosenberg, J. F. (1986). *The Thinking Self.* Philadelphia: Temple University Press.

Rosenthal, D. (1983). "Reductionism and Knowledge." In L. S. Cauman et al. (eds.), *How Many Questions? Essays in Honor of Sidney Morgenbesser.* Indianapolis: Hackett Publishing.

Rosenthal, D. (1986). "Two Concepts of Consciousness." *Philosophical Studies* 94:329–359.

Rosenthal, D. (1990a). "The Colors and Shapes of Visual Experiences." Report no. 28/1990, Research Group on Mind and Brain, Zentrum für Interdisziplinäre Forschung, Bielefeld, Germany.

Rosenthal, D. (1990b). "A Theory of Consciousness." Report no. 40, Research Group on Mind and Brain, Zentrum für Interdisziplinäre Forschung, Bielefeld, Germany.

Rosenthal, D. (1991a). "The Independence of Consciousness and Sensory Quality." In Villanueva 1991.

Rosenthal, D. (1991b). "Explaining Consciousness." Unpublished manuscript presented at the Perspectives on Mind conference, Washington University, December 1991.

Rosenthal, D. (1992). "Thinking That One Thinks." In Davies and Humphreys 1992.

Sanford, D. H. (1981). "Where Was I?" In Hofstadter and Dennett 1981.

Searle, J. (1992). *The Rediscovery of the Mind.* Cambridge: MIT Press.

Sellars, W. (1962). "Philosophy and the Scientific Image of Man." In R. Colodny (ed.), *Frontiers of Science and Philosophy.* Pittsburgh: University of Pittsburgh Press.

Sellars, W. (1965). "The Identity Approach to the Mind-Body Problem. *Review of Metaphysics* 18:430–451.

Sellars, W. (1968). *Science and Metaphysics.* London: Routledge and Kegan Paul.

Sellars, W. (1971). "Science, Sense Impressions, and Sensa: A Reply to Cornman." *Review of Metaphysics* 24:391–447.

Shepard, R. (1990). "A Possible Evolutionary Basis for Trichromacy." In Michael H. Brill (ed.), *Perceiving, Measuring, and Using Color,* Proceedings of SPIE, no. 1250, pp. 301–309. Bellingham, Wash.: Society of Photo-optical Instrumentation Engineers (International Society for Optical Engineering).

Shepard, R. (1991). "Is the Subjective Quality of Conscious Experience a Biological Adaptation?" Unpublished manuscript.

Shepard, R. (1992). "The Perceptual Organization of Colors: An Adaptation to Regularities of the Terrestrial World?" In J. Barkow, L. Cosmides, and J. Tooby (eds.), *The Adapted Mind: Evolutionary Psychology and the Generation of Culture.* Oxford: Oxford University Press.

Shepard, R. (1993). "On the Physical Basis, Linguistic Representation, and Conscious Experience of Colors." In G. Harman (ed.), *Conceptions of the Mind: Essays in Honor of George A. Miller.* Hillsdale, N.J.: Lawrence Erlbaum Associates.

Sheridan, G. (1969). "The Electroencephalogram Argument against Incorrigibility." *American Philosophical Quarterly* 6:62–70.

Shoemaker, S. (1975). "Functionalism and Qualia." *Philosophical Studies* 27:291–315.

Shoemaker, S. (1982). "The Inverted Spectrum." *Journal of Philosophy* 79:357–381.

Shoemaker, S. (1990). "Qualities and Qualia: What's in the Mind?" *Philosophy and Phenomenological Research* 50 (suppl. vol.): 109–131.

Shoemaker, S. (1994a). "Phenomenal Character." *Noûs* 28:21–38.

Shoemaker, S. (1994b). "Self-Knowledge and 'Inner Sense'. Lecture II: The Broad Perceptual Model." *Philosophy and Phenomenological Research* 54:271–290.

Sicha, J. (1991). Review of Lycan, *Consciousness. Noûs* 25:553–561.

Stalnaker, R. (in press). "On a Defense of the Hegemony of Representation." In Villanueva, in press.

Stich, S. P. (1978a). "Autonomous Psychology and the Belief-Desire Thesis." *Monist* 61:573–591. Reprinted in Lycan 1990.

Stich, S. P. (1978b). "Beliefs and Subdoxastic States." *Philosophy of Science* 45:499–519.

Stich, S. P. (1991). "Narrow Content Meets Fat Syntax." In B. Loewer and G. Rey (eds.), *Meaning in Mind: Fodor and His Critics.* Oxford: Basil Blackwell.

Taylor, D. M. (1966). "The Incommunicability of Content." *Mind* 75:527–541.

Teller, P. (1984). "A Poor Man's Guide to Supervenience and Determination." *Southern Journal of Philosophy* 22, suppl.: 137–162.

Teller, P. (1992). "Subjectivity and Knowing What It's Like." In A. Beckermann, H. Flohr, and J. Kim (eds.), *Emergence or Reduction? Essays on the Prospects of Nonreductive Physicalism.* New York: Walter de Gruyter.

Thomason, R. (1973). "Perception and Individuation." In M. Munitz (ed.), *Logic and Ontology.* New York: New York University Press.

Tomberlin, J. E. (1988). "Semantics, Psychological Attitudes, and Conceptual Role." *Philosophical Studies,* 53:205–226.

Tomberlin, J. E. (ed.) (1990). *Action Theory and Philosophy of Mind.* Philosophical Perspectives, no. 4. Atascadero, Calif.: Ridgeview Publishing.

Tye, M. (1986). "The Subjective Qualities of Experience," *Mind* 95:1–17.

Tye, M. (1991). *The Imagery Debate.* Cambridge: MIT Press.

Tye, M. (1992). "Visual Qualia and Visual Content." In Crane 1992.

Tye, M. (1994). "Qualia, Content, and the Inverted Spectrum." *Noûs* 28:159–183.

Tye, M. (1995). "Blindsight, Orgasm, and Representational Overlap." *Behavioral and Brain Sciences* 18:268–269.

Tye, M. (1996). *Ten Puzzles about Consciousness.* Cambridge: MIT Press.

Tye, M. (in press). "Perceptual Representation Is a Many-Layered Thing." In Villaneuva, in press.

Van Gulick, R. (1980). "Functionalism, Information, and Content." *Nature and System* 2:139–162. Reprinted in Lycan 1990.

Van Gulick, R. (1982). "Physicalism and the Subjectivity of the Mental." *Philosophical Topics* 13:51–70.

Van Gulick, R. (1988). "A Functionalist Plea for Self-Consciousness." *Philosophical Review* 97:149–181.

Van Gulick, R. (1989). "What Difference Does Consciousness Make?" *Philosophical Topics* 17:211–230.

Van Gulick, R. (1992). "Understanding the Phenomenal Mind: Are We All Just Armadillos?" In Davies and Humphreys 1992.

Van Gulick, R. (1994). "Deficit Studies and the Function of Phenomenal Consciousness." In G. Graham and L. Stephens (eds.), *Philosophy and Psychopathology.* Cambridge: MIT Press.

Villanueva, E. (ed.) (1991). *Consciousness*. Philosophical Issues, no. 1. Atascadero, Calif.: Ridgeview Publishing.

Villanueva, E. (ed.) (in press). *Philosophical Issues: Perceptual Content*. Atascadero, Calif.: Ridgeview Publishing.

White, S. (1986). "Curse of the Qualia." *Synthese* 68:333–368.

White, S. (1987). "What Is It Like to Be a Homunculus?" *Pacific Philosophical Quarterly* 68:148–174.

Yagisawa, T. (1987). "Yes, You." *Philosophia* 17:169–186.

REFERENCES

Index